HIDDE

BERKSHIRE

CU00500164

HIDDEN

BERKSHIRE

**Compiled by the Berkshire
Federation of Women's Institutes from notes
sent by Institutes in the County**

with illustrations by Pip Challenger

**Published jointly by
Countryside Books, Newbury
and the B.F.W.I., Mortimer**

First Published 1990
© Berkshire Federation of Women's Institutes 1990

COUNTRYSIDE BOOKS
3 Catherine Road
Newbury, Berkshire

ISBN 1 85306 068 2

Typeset by Quad Four Typesetting, Reading
Produced through MRM Associates Ltd., Reading
Printed in England by J. W. Arrowsmith Ltd., Bristol

Foreword

Berkshire is rich in treasures from the past, and who better to tell their stories than the people who live in and love their own patch of this beautiful county. This book has provided Berkshire Federation of Women's Institutes with the opportunity to continue their research, begun with their Berkshire Village Book, into the county's history, this time including both large towns and little-known places too.

It has been a fascinating and absorbing process for W.I. members, their families and friends. Without their work this book would not have been possible. We are grateful to them all, and also to Christine Ingram who co-ordinated the project.

All those who contributed have gained much pleasure from their task. We hope that readers will gain much enjoyment from it too.

Gillian Fricker
County Chairman

HUNGERFORD

NEWBURY

River Kennet

N

MAIDENHEAD

SLOUGH

River Thames

WINDSOR

READING

BRACKNELL

The Royal County of *BERKSHIRE*

Aldermaston's hidden lake

Aldermaston

As the only public house in the village of Aldermaston, the 17th century Hind's Head boasts its own brewhouse, an attractive clock and bell tower. For those supping too freely, beware the dome-roofed gaolhouse close by – although last used in 1865!

The William pear, originally known as the Aldermaston pear, was first propagated by the village schoolmaster, John Staid, in 1840. It is said that a cutting was given to Australia, where it is now known as the Bartlett pear.

The grazing rights of Church Acres, belonging to the church of St Mary the Virgin, are auctioned triennially in December. A horseshoe nail is inserted in a tallow candle one inch below the wick. The bidding begins as the candle is lit, the three-year rights going to the highest bidder as the nail drops out. This is one of the last places in England to continue this ancient custom.

The church of St Mary the Virgin has a Norman door, part of the original 12th century structure and wall paintings, some dating from the early 14th century. The tower has a west window dating from the 15th century. There are five hatchments (the coat of arms of a deceased person, painted on black and hung cornerwise) of the Congrieve family hung on the south and west walls. Two of the eight bells date from 1681.

The church was originally a cell of Pamber Priory, which provided the priest; he rode to the church on a palfrey to say the Mass on Sundays and returned to the priory in the evening.

The York Mystery Cycle, dating from the 14th century, has been staged in the church for over 30 years. The costumes are copies of 14th century English clothing and most have been in use since the first performance. The music is contemporary to the period of the play, including a piece by William Byrd. The Nativity plays for one week to full audiences from near and far.

Not far from the main road in Aldermaston, up the hill out of the village, is a hidden man-made lake. It was constructed by a farmer in 1977-78, following the drought of 1976, to avoid another shortage of water. It has naturalised very well: coots nest there every year, and there are visiting swans, Canada geese, mallard, moorhens, tufted ducks and grebes. It is an ideal peaceful spot for a walk – but few know of its existence.

The following story of the Aldermaston Witch appeared in the WI's Berkshire Book in 1939: 'An old woman, Maria Hale by name, living some 80 years ago, had the power of witchcraft; she would turn herself into a large brown hare and haunt the park [Aldermaston] where she lived in a cottage. The hare was never killed, but a local keeper shot her, wounding her in the leg. Ever after it was noticed that Maria Hale was lame. As a hare she would sit outside the Fuzz Bush (the local name for the Falcon Inn), and as Maria Hale she always knew who had visited there. No dog would ever chase the brown hare.

'As a witch she was greatly feared in the village. One day she demanded of the village shopkeeper that he would buy two flitches of bacon that she had. Very unwillingly he went with her to her cottage, where she made him follow her upstairs to the bedroom. There between the mattresses of her bed lay the two fine flitches, which the poor man was forced to buy. They say that never was such good bacon tasted in the village, yet Maria Hale kept no pigs!

'She would lean over garden gates and ask for flowers, and if they were refused her she would bewitch the plant, which would die. She even bewitched her own son, when he wanted to go and work in Windsor. Against her wish he left the village, but was soon home again, having fallen sick. He recovered immediately he returned.

'When she died Maria Hale was buried under the yew tree in the churchyard. The man who helped his father dig her grave, tells how the coffin was rammed down with stones and bricks so that the witch should not rise again.

'These stories were told me in all seriousness by a 75 year old inhabitant, and are confirmed by several village contemporaries.'

Ashmore Green

Before the erection of the small Baptist chapel in Ashmore Green, services were held in a large old cottage, where the occupants were very poor and could afford little firing. Those who attended the services were also poor, so were unable to help, but the cottage was always so full that the men had to stand. The very first service was conducted by one Benjamin Josey. The services were later attended by Mr Thomas Clayton, who kept a china shop in Cheap Street, Newbury, and Mr G. C. Taylor, also from Newbury, who eventually informed the congregation that they had purchased a plot of land on which to build a chapel. The cost of the land was 30 shillings. This news naturally delighted the locals.

Messrs Clayton and Taylor then came to Ashmore Green to collect money for the building of the chapel, the very first donation being one farthing from a child playing in the village. Further monies were collected at the cottage services, and the new chapel was eventually opened for worship just before Christmas 1866. Two weeks later Mr Clayton started a Sunday school, and at one time a total of 53 children attended.

Soon the chapel was not large enough. Mr Alfred Pocock donated land for an extension, and Granny Franklin and her girls again went around the district collecting. Friends from outside the Fellowship were very generous, particularly the teachers from Barrier Bank chapel.

Later, the vestry, stable and coach house at the rear were converted into a schoolroom, thanks to the Superintendent, Mr H. D. Mayers, who ran the school from 1893 until 1940, when he was succeeded by his daughter, Miss Daisy Mayers, who continued the good work until 1956. One pupil, a product of the Sunday school, was the Rev Walter Fullbrook, who trained for the Baptist Ministry at Spurgeons College, and later, with his wife, did missionary work in the Congo.

After 95 years of witness, the building became unsafe for worship and, after an unsuccessful search for a new site, the old chapel was closed in 1961. It has since become a museum for the late Mr Reg Piper's collection of mechanical musical instruments.

David Piper, known locally as Barty, was born in 1838 and spent most of his life in the Ashmore Green area. At the age of 16 he volunteered for service in the militia and served in the Crimean War.

It was during his military service that drink and all the evils associated with it took hold of him and, after leaving the service, he went from bad to worse. He was known locally as a demon fighter and was more than a match for any two men.

Often his wife, Mary Ann, would go out searching for him to secure what money he had left to buy food for the children. She often had to drag him home after he had been drinking and on one occasion carried him four miles on her back.

As a poacher, which was his way of living, Barty was daring and clever and not once was he caught. He was shrewd, keen-eyed and alert and although he followed this dangerous pattern of life for almost half a century, he was only in the hands of the police on one occasion and that was for fighting in the Market Place in Newbury.

After a fight with two men at Shaw he had to be helped home by a lady from the Salvation Army. Unable to read or write, he heard of the conversion of a poacher related in the *War Cry*. He asked for it to be read to him again and it caused him considerable agitation of the mind. Following another meeting, whilst working in the woods, he had a direct revelation from God, and kneeling there gave himself fully to Him. Converted, he then spent many years revisiting the public houses speaking of the evils of drink. He was taken ill at a meeting in the Citadel and had to be taken home, where he died. He had served the Salvation Army for 28 years.

His body was laid to rest at St Mark's, Cold Ash, on 26th April 1910 and the Corps joined the funeral procession, where the greatest crowd ever seen had collected to show respect.

Barkham

Barkham is the oldest village in the locality and has fought to retain its own individuality against the large housing estates that have sprung up around it. It is mentioned in the Domesday Book and was the boundary of Henry VIII's deer hunting forest. The name Barkham is thought to derive from the silver birch copses. The local woods are still full of deer, badgers, foxes and other wild life.

St James' church stands on a site used for worship since the days when a visiting monk would cross the downs from Newbury. The chalice dates from the reign of Charles I. During the time of Oliver Cromwell it was hidden with all the church silver in the village pond and was recovered when the pond was drained in the reign of Charles II.

The cedar tree in the churchyard is over 200 years old. It is now unfortunately feeling its age, but has bravely withstood the worst of the gales. Also in the churchyard is the grave of George Washington's grandmother. The church in recent times has had a new wing built on by the generosity of the Walter family.

John Walter was the founder of *The Times* newspaper, and he lived in a fine mansion where Bearwood College now stands. He was responsible for the building of many local church halls and schools. The third John Walter tragically lost his eldest son in a skating accident on Bearwood Lake. The young man made a brave attempt to save his cousin who had gone through the ice and lost his own life in doing so. A daughter of the family also died when very young and the church at Bearwood was dedicated to St Catherine in her memory.

Barkham was a fine village with a rectory, glebe lands, manor house, village green and public house. The forge, by the side of the Bull public house, was in use until fairly recently. Often several horses would be tethered outside awaiting their turn for shoeing. There are at least two sets of moat houses in the area; the church cottages at Barkham and cottages in Swallowfield Lane, and also the Moat House near Arborfield Camp, which has now been filled in.

The ancient oak tree at the Coppid Hill Garage was thought to be at least 400 years old. Unfortunately it blew down in October 1987. The base of the tree would have made a large dining table!

The surrounding countryside is still very beautiful, with farmlands and fields, full of young lambs in spring and alight with the crimson glow of poppies in summer. Most of the hedgerows are ancient, containing many different types of trees and bushes, though these are now under threat from development.

California is a man-made lake and the site for a holiday camp owned by Wokingham Council. The lake abounds with water birds and is beautiful in summer with water lilies and surrounding banks of rhododendrons.

Beenham

As you take a walk down one of the many public footpaths in Beenham, you may be surprised to come across a caged area containing wolves. They are as inquisitive as you, as you walk by, quietly hoping they cannot escape.

A talk with Mrs Palmer, who, with her husband, owns these magnificent creatures, will soon put your mind at rest. The wolves are the only tame wolves in Europe, and are used for many film and television programmes and television commercials.

They are often seen walking on leads through the village with their owners; although they are shy timid creatures, if approached with a friendly coaxing voice they will let you stroke them.

However, on a cold winter afternoon just before dark, the sound of their howling can send a chill down your spine – until you realise they only want their tea!

St Mary's Farm was, until the 1950s, the parsonage house for Beenham church. One of the vicars who lived in an earlier version of the house that stands today was Thomas Stackhouse, the author of *The History of the Bible from the Beginning of the World until the Coming of Christianity*, which he wrote in 1792. At the time he was famous as a theologian; today he is perhaps better remembered locally for his reputation as a very heavy drinker.

The present building was substantially altered and enlarged in the late Georgian period. At the back of the house are three bricks bearing the date 1825, and the initials of various members of the Bushnell family, who were vicars of this parish for four generations. The handsome stone tomb in the churchyard, on the north side of the tower, is the Bushnell's vault. This family almost certainly planted the large ilex on the top lawn, the Scots pine in the hollow of the field and the walnut in the centre of the garden. The apple tree on the lowest level of the lawn may well have been part of the Bushnell's orchard, which apparently stretched into the field for about 100 yards.

From the house a narrow path between high hedges leads all the way down to the church. This was the vicar's walk and it is a fascinating example of a late 18th century shrub walk. Among the hollies are laburnums and a few old roses, which were favourite flowering shrubs in the Georgian period. It is likely that lilacs and philadelphus would also have grown there and the present owners of the house are planning to restore this walk, now that the rest of the garden has been established. Apart from the odd modern plant the aim here has been to recreate the garden of a country rectory.

Visitors to St Mary's church have a panoramic view of the Kennet valley. In the churchyard many fine old tombstones can be found, one bearing a trumpeting angel bestowing a crown, another Father Time with his scythe.

The oldest legible tombstone is in memory of Jane, wife of Robert Webb, who died on 7th April 1745.

> 'My head, my hands, my heart, my mind,
> With all their might sought God to find.
> And now I am forever blessed,
> For with my Jesus I have rest.
> All ye who read these lines take care
> Or else you'd have no portion there.'

Inside the church are eight frescoes and a most beautiful painting of the Last Supper, all painted by Miss Sharp of Ufton Nervet.

The Winning Hand pub, built at the turn of the century, started its life as a place of ill-repute! Until 1987 called 'The Emerald Lady', it had been variously a tea-room, an inn and a guest house. Now it is best known as a restaurant, and has been extensively redecorated and refurbished. It is situated just off the Bath Road.

The Six Bells dates from the 18th century, and is in the older part of Beenham. When the parish church was destroyed by fire in 1794, villagers collected enough melted ball metal in the churchyard to reduce the replacement bill for the bells very considerably, and the Six Bells was given its name following that event.

The landlord of that time, Walter Applebee, left in his will £5 to each of his two brothers; 13 years later, in 1808, he reduced the amount to five shillings. We are not told what the brothers did to reduce their expectations!

The Hare and Hounds is a 17th century inn. Standing on the important Bath Road, the main highway to the West, it was originally known as 'The Halfway', being equidistant not only from Reading and Newbury, but also Beenham and Padworth. A milestone stands nearby, depicting the boundary between these two parishes. No-one knows why the name was changed, or whether there was actually a hunting connection.

Binfield

In 1989 a hidden garden came to light in Binfield. Its crumbling pillars, dry pools and overgrown shrubs had lain almost undisturbed for decades behind the neo-Tudor mansion of Moor Close.

Moor Close was built originally in the 1880s. When the middle-aged millionaire owner, Charles Birch Crisp, discovered to his delight that he was to become a father he named his new garden, planned and built in 1910-1911, after his new baby – Sylvia's Garden. The birth was an event which no doubt made an impression on many people living nearby, for Crisp also handed out a gold sovereign to everyone working on his estate.

The garden was designed by Oliver Hill, who became one of Britain's most celebrated architects. A focal point was the magnificent pergola and colonnade, and from many places along the garden walks could be glimpsed views of the surrounding countryside. During the 1920s the garden was a meeting place of the rich and famous, including Lloyd George and the Prince of Wales.

Crisp eventually ran into financial difficulties and the estate was sold in the 1930s. The present owner of Moor Close, who bought the house in 1945, is the Seventh Day Adventist Church, and it is known as Newbold College.

When it was realised how near the gardens were to disappearing for ever, an appeal was launched. Sylvia's Garden will eventually be restored to its former glory, and will be open to the public at certain times. Its revival is being overseen by Paul Edwards, who restored the gardens at Warwick Castle.

Opposite Moor Close is the church of All Saints, much of it dating from the 15th century. There is a fascinating 17th century hourglass stand by the pulpit, which carries the arms of the Farriers' Company of London – a wolf, a lion, a pelican, leaves and grapes. Another treasure is under the carpet in the chancel, a nine inch brass memorial to Walter de Anneforde, which is possibly the oldest brass in Berkshire, dating from about 1360. It is a palimpsest, which means that it has been used again, as shown by the discovery of 16th century inscriptions and the outline of an abbot or bishop.

On the south wall is a marble tablet in memory of Catherine Macaulay Graham, who died in 1791. She moved here after marrying William Graham, a second marriage after a life which had taken her far from her birthplace at Wye. She was a respected historian and writer, and was particularly noted for her eight volume *History of England* which was published between 1763 and 1783.

Boxford

'A village is quiet, its cottages are the storehouses of past memories. Within their walls nothing is forgotten. There stays an echo of past moments.'

(From *The Quiet Village* by Ursula Bloom)

There are homes in Boxford which have withstood rain and sun for 300 or 400 years. One or two of the very ancient cottages, such as Stream Cottage in Westbrook, Heath Cottage and Oliver's Cottage, were of 'cruck' construction, as was Ivy Cottage near the chapel. Cruck is an Anglo Saxon word for 'bent'. A tree would be felled and its branches lopped. Then the trunk would be split in two so that the tops curved inwards towards a huge central beam, supporting both walls and roof, the axe marks still on it as the day it was felled. Windows then were 'wind holes' or 'wind eyes' and had no coverings. Early homes were very dark inside and from this came the saying, 'Never darken my door again'. Many of the interior beams of Boxford's thatched cottages came from ships' timbers.

The church of St Andrew has a wonderful list recording the names of rectors from 1190. It begins: '1190 – Ricardus Clericus', who was a monk from Abingdon. In the early 1800s barrel organs were much in vogue and Boxford church has one of these instruments – one of only 30 or so remaining in the country. This organ has five barrels and a range of 50 hymns or songs. It can still be induced to 'make a joyful noise unto the Lord' but not so musically as of old.

The earliest Boxfordians could have been of the Middle Stone Age, making their exploratory journey along what is known now as the Lambourn river. Few traces of their material culture have been discovered, but the Later Stone Age men left eight flint scrapers to come to light.

Found at Westbrook Farm too was a flint saw of this period, and another scraper, whilst at Ownham Farm a rough flint hoe was unearthed. The site of a Roman villa was excavated just off the Boxford—Winterbourne road and pottery and coins have been found here by labourers. Potsherds of Romano-British origin, roof tiles (one with the imprint of a sandalled foot), and a pot about twelve

Brook Cottage, Boxford

20

inches high holding 800 coins (now in Newbury Museum),
has also been found. The coins were stamped with the
heads of five Emperors. A Roman 'glave' or 'short sword'
was also dug up locally, and a lady in the village has a
brooch, found in Boxford, which she believes to be Roman.

Bracknell

◄━━ There has been a settlement here for many centuries, named 'Braccen Heal' in the early 10th century. It has
been suggested that the name may have connections with
a holy spring or well. There are many springs in Bracknell
and there is a Holly Spring Lane on the north side of the
town. Could this have been the Holy Well of the past?

In the early 19th century Bracknell was just a rural
wayside hamlet, though even then there were some attractive large houses nearby, such as Easthampstead Park.
Then it began to grow, and in 1946 it was named as an area
of development under the New Towns Act. The streets in
the neighbourhood of Great Hollands off Ringmead were
named alphabetically (Abbotsbury, Ambassador, Apple-
dore etc) after old London telephone exchanges. It is said
to have been done to make the Londoners who came to live
here feel at home.

At the top of what was once Bracknell High Street, now
known as Grenville Place, and part of the pedestrian
precinct, stands 'Whynscar', a house built in 1760 and now
surrounded by modern buildings. Formerly a private
house, though in 1930 antiques were sold from it, it has
now been converted, fairly 'sympathetically' to offices.
The last private owner who moved there in 1952 was a
dentist, who had his surgery there. It was he and his wife
who discovered a priest hole and baking oven in the
fireplace of their dining room, and another was found later

by builders, between two bedrooms – the solution to why the walls did not appear to abut.

In the 17th and 18th centuries, the house was known as 'Dick Turpin's Cottage', and there are underground passages which led to a nearby hostelry - now pulled down and replaced by Bracknell College of Further Education!

Bracknell College is also on the site of the old cattle and poultry market, established in 1870 behind the Hinds Head Hotel, and when the old Priestwood primary school closed down, less than a mile away, it was taken over by one of the College faculties.

Just before the old school, at the junction of Downshire Way and Binfield Road, is the old graveyard of the Primitive Methodist chapel.

The size of the graveyard – no bigger than a room in a house – suggests that it was once part of a larger plot. This is not so. The Primitive Methodists (so called as a reference to their style of unsophisticated worship in its early and original form) did not stay long in the area. The dates on the headstones suggest 1820-1860.

It is known that by 1888 St Andrew's church was built in the Binfield Road, on land behind Edwards Store which now has Boyd Court flats, and it is unlikely that the small community could support the two churches, bearing in mind that other parish boundaries were already drawn . There is no trace of either church building now.

St Anthony's Children's Home overlooks the road junction. The bedroom of some of the senior lads looked out at the graveyard and school and often they would lie awake telling each other ghost stories which included the graveyard over yonder.

There have been occasional attempts to buy it up and round off the corner, but, although unattended and overgrown, it is still there.

The parish church of Holy Trinity, Bracknell, was built by public subscription, and completed in 1851, on land formerly owned and donated by Lord Braybrooke. The new parish of Bracknell was formed from parts of Easthampstead, Winkfield and Warfield parishes, and, until 1966 the vicar was known as 'The perpetual curate of Winkfield'.

Canon Barnett, who lived in Larges Lane, and after whom Barnett Court, sheltered accommodation in the lane, is named, did a great deal for the interior of the church. He also introduced communion once a week, where it had previously been celebrated once a month. In the south transept of the church, an unusual stained-glass window shows St Birinus holding a model of Dorchester Abbey, with the face of the Canon.

Now within the bounds of Bracknell New Town is the ancient village of Easthampstead. The old manor house was originally a hunting lodge, since this was part of Windsor Forest, and the present house was only built in the 1860s by the Marquis of Downshire. The Downshire influence is apparent in other buildings in the old village, including the church of St Michael and St Mary Magdalene, and Church Hill House Hospital. The latter began life as almshouses, which became the union workhouse in 1826 and has now developed into a   residential hospital for the handicapped.

There is an old story in Easthampstead, said to date from the 17th century, of a miller who turned away from his door a poor man dressed in rags. It was a hard winter and the miller, a notoriously mean man, had ignored all appeals for help from his less fortunate neighbours. The poor beggar, unable to go any farther without food, collapsed and died outside the miller's door. From then on the miller knew no peace. His crops failed, his livestock died and he was haunted by a thin figure dressed in rags. Finally the miller himself was forced to go begging on the road, his livelihood gone. The villagers of Easthampstead burned his mill to the ground and the ghostly beggar was seen no more.

Bradfield

An unusual weather vane can be seen on Bradfield college chapel – it depicts a schoolmaster in cap and gown and is in memory of Dr Gray, who was headmaster from 1880 to 1910. It was made in 1951 by the village blacksmith, Frank Ford.

In Southend, Bradfield, on a farm building you can see another delightful vane which cleverly combines the ancient name of Boot Farm with the fairly recent riding school run by the daughter of the family. It is in the shape of a jodhpur boot and was designed by a friend, Mrs Draper, and made in 1984 by a local iron worker, Norman Cameron.

A little way up a track from Back Lane there is a large old barn, known locally as the Black Barn as it has for many years had a black corrugated iron roof – no doubt replacing the original thatch. It is a beautiful old structure of uncertain date, and as well as being used for farm purposes, it serves as a rural meeting place for harvest lunches, village barn dances, etc by kind permission of Rushall Farm. Other old farm buildings round it are now used by the John Simonds Trust for young people to gain experience of country living and crafts.

The names of several roads in the village are reminders of the past. Scratchface Lane speaks for itself. It is no longer as narrow as it must have been when it was first named, but still is quite a problem for the motorist who meets a farm tractor.

Union Road gets its name from one of the first workhouses (or Unions as they were often called) which was built in 1835. The building with its fine frontage is at present known as Wayland Hospital (because the surrounding field and copse had that name) but its future as a home for mentally handicapped people is in doubt, as more and more of the inhabitants are being accommodated elsewhere 'in the community'.

Cock Lane was so called because it starts from the inn which was originally known as 'The Cock and Breeches', though since the early 1800s at least it has been the Queen's Head.

The Gas House is now a private house but with its remarkable frontage preserved. It can best be seen across the fields from the old mill, now part of Bradfield College. It was built by Thomas Stevens, the founder of the college, in 1867 to provide lighting for the school and other buildings nearby.

In St Andrew's church a particularly interesting piece of stone carving can be seen on the two pillars of the sanctuary at the east end of the church. If you look carefully you can see a swallow and a sparrow, and find the reference in Psalm 84: 'Yea, the sparrow hath found an house, and the swallow a nest for herself, where she may lay her young, even thine altars, O Lord of hosts, my king and my God.'

The church itself is 14th century, but was rebuilt in the 19th century by Gilbert Scott under the patronage of the lord of the manor, Thomas Stevens.

Brimpton

When renovations were taking place at Manor Farm, behind the modern fireplace and nine others, the original beamed fireplace was discovered. But even more exciting was the discovery in the huge chimney breast, of a priest's hole, a reminder of the troubled times of the 16th and 17th centuries. Hopefully, a priest only needed to hide in the summer! Manor Farm also has a Knights Templar chapel in its grounds, the chapel of St Leonard. This small flint building has a Norman doorway.

Another discovery in the village was a well, from which water had been drawn by pump for many years. It was found in the middle of the kitchen floor of the house attached to the village shop, known as Forge Stores. This well never ran dry even in the longest spells of drought. When all other neighbouring sources of water had dried up, the farmers were still able to get water for their cattle from this well. The importance of reliable sources of water cannot be over- emphasised in the everyday life of village people. Many villages did not have a mains water supply until the 1950s.

A splendid oak tree dominates a small triangular area of land right in the centre of Brimpton village. Behind it a track leads up to St Peter's church, by its side is the war memorial, and beneath it is a seat commemorating the Silver Jubilee of our present Queen.

This oak was planted as a young sapling in 1887 to mark the Golden Jubilee of Queen Victoria. It has now become a very worthy and impressive landmark to a great Queen.

Crookham Common, not far from the village of Brimpton was, in the past, a well known collecting place for the 'travelling' or gipsy people. There are many stories of fights and confrontations with the local people. The public house by the common is called the Traveller's Friend.

Each year a horse fair was held in the field next to a house called Old Thatch. Here, the travellers and others met to buy and sell horses, and the field was reported to be full of caravans and tents at this time. No doubt some of the

26

deals were very 'interesting', especially to the unwary buyer!

In 1831 a corn merchant named Jabez Vines took a lease of Brimpton Mill. He was a member of the Baptists in Reading. Each Sunday, he and his family and friends met together in the mill house, for prayers and praise, and he read a sermon to them. Other people in the village were attracted to the meetings, and Jabez Vines decided to license the mill house for public worship. Later, a Sunday school was formed.

Influential local people tried to prevent the growth of the Baptists and refused to sell them land on which to build a chapel. But in 1837 John Goddard, a local yeoman farmer who had joined them, provided a piece of land for a small sum and the present chapel and manse were built. The first baptisms took place in the river close to the mill, in 1843.

Burchetts Green

Hall Place was built in the mid 1700s for a wealthy Londoner called William East. Today the red brick mansion is used by the Berkshire College of Agriculture. There are some fascinating reminders of the past, including the remains of a cockpit, but perhaps the most unusual of all is the beehouse.

For many hundreds of years bees were kept in straw skeps. These needed protection from the weather, either individually or more usually by a beehouse. When the movable-frame wooden beehives came into use, from the 1860s, they continued to be installed in beehouses much as the skeps had been previously. Later it was found that it was much more convenient to give hives an individual roof and make them free standing. Beehouses then (almost) went out of use and disappeared.

The Beehouse at Burchetts Green

The beehouse at Hall Place was built about 1870. (It is possible that it was a re-build of a much earlier house incorporating the central pillar.) It is a ten-sided building, having a door in one side and places for one hive in each of the other nine sides. The lattice work near the base and just below the eaves is backed with perforated zinc to allow adequate ventilation. By 1960 the structure was deteriorating due to the movement of the foundations caused by the roots of adjacent trees. Some repair kept it intact until 1979, when a complete restoration was effected. As much of the original as possible was re-used including floor, step, brickwork, central pillar, central benching, much of the roof timber, beehives and stands and even the catches of the windows. It is probably the finest example of a beehouse of this period in England. It is approximately 14 feet in diameter.

Caversham

👉 Until 1911 Caversham was in Oxfordshire, with the Thames forming a useful boundary between it and the growing town of Reading. It had become a residential suburb of the town even then, but the merging of the old village into the borough of Reading was strongly, albeit unsuccessfully, resisted by the residents of Caversham. In 1926 the new Caversham Bridge over the Thames brought the village even closer to Reading.

St Peter's church dates back to Norman times and contains a Norman font carved out of Purbeck marble. It stood close to the old 17th century rectory, Caversham Court, which has been demolished, though the Court gardens still overlook the Thames.

At the top of Priest Hill in Caversham, at the junction with St Anne's Road, sits St Anne's Well. It was an important place of pilgrimage during the Middle Ages, attracting travellers with a variety of afflictions from far and wide. It had strong connections with the 13th century Chapel of St Anne, Mother of Our Lady, which used to stand on Caversham Bridge. Before visiting the well, pilgrims would stop here to see the holy relics brought to Caversham, it is said, by an angel with one wing.

Chaddleworth

👉 The following is an extract from *History of Chaddleworth* written by R.S. Mosdell, dated 7th April 1914. However, this is probably a copy of an earlier work by an unknown author, perhaps a teacher at the dame school, as in another part of the account mention is made of 'the building of two new cottages last year (1855), but not yet occupied', and there are no entries relating to events after this date.

'The living of Chaddleworth was given, together with the manor of Poughley, to the Dean and Chapter of Westminster by Henry VIII in exchange for 100 acres of land, St James' Park, London.

'At a place anciently called Ellenfordesmere in the parish of Chaddleworth, there was a hermit in very early times. In the year 1160 a priory for the regular canons of the Order of St Augustine was founded on the spot where the hermitage had stood, by Ralph de Chaddlewoth, who dedicated it to St Margaret. The meadow adjoining the priory still retains the name of Margaret's Mead.

'The place was then called Poghill or Pogchele, and in the reign of Edward IV was endowed with £50 per annum. It was one of the small monasteries dissolved by Wolsey at that time [ie the 1500s]. The annual value was £91.10s.7d.

'It is supposed that in early times there was a town around Poughley, which has in some measure been confirmed by large stones and bricks being ploughed up at different times on the lands belonging to the farm. It is also reported that Margaret's Mead is laid with stones about a yard below the surface, and was the old market place. The materials of the priory (stones etc) were used many years ago in building barn walls and outhouses on the farm, but part of the foundation of the chapel is still visible.

'In the year 1797 a very large heap of earth lying at the back of the Farmhouse was moved and thrown into pits about the farm, many skulls and bones were found and carted away with it.

'The men employed in moving the stones in the Chapel found a larger stone slab, lying even with the floor, about five and a half feet in length, two feet in width, and four inches thick. A cross and letters in bas-relief were carved thereon. It was probably some relation of Robert Poore, who was Bishop of Salisbury in the 12th century, and it is likely the said person was prior or monk of Poughley.

'The stone was presented as a relic to Mr Eyston of Hendred a few years ago by Mr Wroughton'.

A piscina which, by local repute, came from Poughley priory was found in the garden of a 17th century cottage in the village. It has been put to good use as a herb trough!

Cold Ash

On 18th January 1881, Cold Ash residents woke to a white world with snow so deep that the postman could not make his way through the choked lanes to the upland heights. Still the snow fell in volleying gusts from the dark sky, and was piled by the fierce winds into gigantic drifts that reached the tops of the hedges. Cold Ash was in a state of siege.

In a solitary cottage on the hill lived a carter called George Hawkins who, on that terrible day had gone with his wagon and team to some place miles distant. The roads were dreadful, and for many hours, during which he was without food, he battled desperately against the snow and storm. At length, he could drive his wagon no further, and leaving it in a place of safety for the night, he unharnessed the horses and started to lead them homewards. The short, dark winter day drew quickly to a close, darkness fell, and along the heights of the Ridge which he had to traverse, the wind, thick with swirling flakes, swept fiercely about him.

Only 150 yards separated him from his own doorstep, but his strength was failing him fast. At length, overpowered, he cleared a space of snow, and here his own son found him next morning, frozen to death, the patient horses standing unharmed beside him.

The exact spot of this tragedy was for many years

marked by a simple cross carved into the mossy bank, but unfortunately with the passing of roadside ditches and the removal of the hedge, this sign has been lost for ever.

George Hawkins was laid to rest in the burial ground of St Mark's church, Cold Ash on 26th January 1881, at the age of 40.

In 1886, a property known as Hill House, situated at the junction of The Ridge and the Hermitage Road, was opened as a home for girls rescued from immoral surroundings. A committee was formed and supporters raised money to purchase the house for the Church of England Children's Society, in 1890. A school was opened at its inception as an Industrial School, and in consequence was open to inspection by HM Inspector of Prisons.

The old stable block was converted into a laundry and a quaint little chapel was formed in the stable loft. There was a good deal of land around the property, which provided fresh vegetables, and also space for recreation. The children eligible for St Mary's included those found begging in the street, or found wandering without a home or proper guardianship; also children who were orphaned or had a surviving parent in prison could be accommodated. Children with physical or mental disabilities were not accepted. Later, the children attended the village school, but they had to attend chapel and carry out a task before going to school.

After the Second World War, St Mary's became a home for younger children, many illegitimate, left by returning Forces. The nurses, in smart uniforms with starched white caps, were accepted for nursery nurses' training, although only a part of the training could be undertaken at Cold Ash. Family grouping was then introduced, in an attempt to achieve something like family life, but the nursery remained the domain of women only.

In 1973, St Mary's became an assisted community home,

working in partnership with the Berkshire County Council. The staff came out of the familiar uniforms, and male nurses were admitted. To enable children to integrate more fully with village children, a playgroup was set up, and this was very successful for a number of years.

It came as a great shock when it was announced that the Home was to be closed, and its doors were finally closed on 31st August 1980. The house was converted to four large dwellings, and the children's paddock accommodates five small bungalows.

Also in 1886, a private residence at Cold Ash was converted by a private benefactress to a small cottage hospital for crippled children. The building occupied a high rural site among pine woods. Its role as a hospital changed with the passage of time, but in 1960 there were about 30 child patients, generally with respiratory complaints such as bronchitis, asthma an bronchiectasis. About half the children admitted were from the Reading area. The average length of stay at the hospital was three to twelve months, but some long-stay patients spent as much as five years at Cold Ash.

From very early years a special school operated at the hospital, and in 1917 a lady governess was appointed. The school continued until 1949, when, on the advent of the National Health Service, it was taken over by the Berkshire County Council. The Chairman of the Hospital House Committee was also the Chairman of the Board of Governors of the school.

In Cold Ash a body of people known as the Friends of the Children's Hospital raised money locally, and helped in many other ways with the day-to-day running of the hospital. During and after the Second World War American servicemen from Greenham Common adopted the hospital and were great benefactors, particularly at Christmas time.

Sadly, the hospital closed in 1964 and later was demolished, and the development known as Sewell Close was erected on the land. However, most of the nurses married local men and a great number still reside in Cold Ash. In June 1986 a nostalgic reunion of as many nurses as could be contacted took place.

On the evening of Sunday 15th December 1940, the Acland family of Thirtover House had just settled down to dinner. Present were Lady Acland, who, at that time had reached her 80th year, her daughter Ruth and guests.

Their meal came to an abrupt end when a high-explosive bomb crashed through the roof of Thirtover. The bomb tore through the bedroom and drawing-room, smashing the grand piano and embedding itself in the floor below. Fortunately, it did not explode.

Lady Acland showed great courage, walking to her neighbour's house without assistance. Three other bombs fell in the vicinity, causing nearby houses to be evacuated, and preventing Ashmore Green children from attending the village school the following day.

Ruth Acland, who was a concert singer, and conducted small local choirs, had a baton made from pieces of her grand piano.

Curridge

'Hidden' is an ideal description of Curridge's primary school. It is quite central to the village, yet invisible behind trees for most of the year. Both its history and appearance are unusual.

In 1856 the sisters of John Wasey of Prior's Court, Chieveley, Miss Mary Wasey and Mrs Jane Stackpole, leased some land from the Dean and Chapter of Westminster, and put up a building to be used as both school and

Curridge village school

church for Curridge. The architect was S.S. Teulon, the designer of the Royal Lodge Chapel at Windsor, among other local buildings.

The Education Act of 1870 meant that the school was inspected regularly and the grant allowed depended on the reports made. In 1873 the Board suggested that it would take over and build a new school in another part of the village. This did not suit Miss Wasey, so she paid to keep the school going until her death in 1880. A very uncertain period followed, but the school survived.

Log book entries date back to 1879 and give an insight into the life of a small Berkshire village, largely affected by farming and the weather. It shows a lot, too, concerning the education of over 70 children, learning in an area 29 ft by 17 ft before the first extension in the 1880s.

Until about 1965, the building was transformed into a church on Sundays, which meant quite a lot of furniture moving. It was then deconsecrated and the stained glass

35

windows removed, with the church moving to the ecclesiastical parish of Hermitage.

Various additions to the school have been made in the last 100 years, the latest being in matching style to the original, so Curridge school remains an attractive, as well as useful, item in Hidden Berkshire.

Datchet

William the Conqueror granted the manors of Ditton and Datchet to William, son of Ansculf. In 1472 they became crown land and in 1536 Ditton Park was granted to Anne Boleyn as part of a land settlement on her from Henry VIII. Charles I granted in trust the manors of Datchet and Datchet St Helens to Sir Charles Harbord. Eventually they were sold in 1742 to the 2nd Duke of Montagu, who had inherited Ditton Park in 1709. In 1895 the estate passed to Henry Lord Montagu of Beaulieu, the present Lord Montagu's grandfather.

The manor house at Datchet, with its plaster cat chasing a mouse on the roof, is today a divided residence. It has never been lived in by the present lord of the manor and an antiques business is now carried on there. The new front of 1895 is similar to an old print showing the Elizabethan gables, and the adjoining Manor Cottages which are older were probably stables.

Ditton Manor exists today as Ditton Park. It was purchased from the Montagu family in 1917 by the Admiralty in order that the Compass Department could move out of London away from the magnetic interference caused by the electric trams. For over 60 years that part of Ditton Park not used by the Admiralty Compass Observatory has been the scene of investigations into problems of radio propagation and upper atmosphere research. From the mid

1960s the growing importance of space activities was reflected in the new name, Radio and Space Research Station. In 1979 the laboratory buildings were taken over by the Calor Gas Company.

The manor of Riding Court was owned by Sir Maurice Berkley in 1544 and in 1586 by Richard Hanbury, whose monuments are in the parish church. The property is now a thriving market garden.

The manor of St Helen's was land along the Southlea Road which belonged to the Priory of St Helen's, Bishopsgate, London, in the 14th century. The Priory was dissolved in 1540 and now St Helen's is the name of a field on the Southlea Farm where there are fragments of the wall of the monastery.

Being on the main road from London to Windsor, royalty used the ferry at the end of Datchet High Street from 1249 until Queen Anne had the first timber bridge erected in 1706. The second bridge built in 1770 of timber and stone pillars became unsafe in 1795 and George III supplied a free ferry. In 1811 the Crown legally compelled the Counties of Berkshire and Buckinghamshire to construct a bridge jointly. They could not agree on design or materials, so each built half the bridge to the parish boundary, ie the centre of the river. The Buckinghamshire half was of wood and that of Berkshire was of iron!

In 1848 the railway extension from Richmond to Datchet was opened, teminating at Black Potts Island. The first journey took 85 minutes and was welcomed by large crowds at every station on the 14 mile route. In 1849 the Prince Consort negotiated with the railway company to extend the line across the Home Park into Windsor. The Datchet Bridge was removed, being the only bridge on the Thames to be completely demolished, and in 1851 the Victoria Bridge into Windsor and the Albert Bridge into Old Windsor were built.

The toll gate opposite the Royal Stag was cleared away in 1863 and instead of the regular run of the horse coach from London to Windsor the railway line operated and was electrified in 1930. The May's Crossing received its name from one early crossing keeper who had operated the gates by hand and was finally knocked down by a train. The Queen's Road leading from this crossing to the river is said to be so called because Queen Victoria used it in order to avoid the onlookers when she was held up by an oncoming train.

In Domesday Book Datchet is said to have had two fisheries, producing 2,000 eels. Charles II used to fish here and Alexander Pope wrote:-

'Methinks I see our mighty monarch stand,
The pliant rod now trembling in his hand;
And see, he now doth up from Datchet come
Laden with spoils of slaughter'd gudgeon
home.'

William Shakespeare mentions Datchet in his play *The Merry Wives of Windsor* when Falstaff is hidden in a soiled linen basket for despatch to the laundress at Datchet and is thrown into the river at Datchet Mead.

About 1874 dredging was taking place near the old ford at Datchet and an Eton College master, Mr Samuel Evans was watching to see whether anything of interest would be found. He was lucky - the dredger brought up a Celtic bronze fibula - a brooch for pinning clothing in place. It is in exceptionally good condition, almost four inches long, with seven amber and two blue glass beads. The hinge works perfectly today. The brooch may have been lost during a river crossing or perhaps thrown into the Thames as an offering to a river god. The fibula is in the Myers Museum at Eton College. Also dredged from the river at about the same time were two 'eyed' spear heads, 22 inches long, and a remarkable spear head with gold studs. These are preserved in the British Museum.

The church of St Mary the Virgin, rebuilt in 1857, is surmounted by an unusual octagonal tower with spire and clock. Inside there are some beautiful stained glass windows, including three memorials to HRH Prince Consort. A tablet records the death of Robert Barker and his printing of the Authorised version of the Bible in 1611.

St Mary's C of E school was built in 1844 for the education of the poor, on a site donated by Lord Montagu and the Duke of Buccleuch. A valuable document handed down by the headmasters is the school log which dates from 1854. It records the attendances - affected by epidemics, severe winters and flooding, also the visits of royalty to the village. Also recorded is the landing by Sir Thomas Sopwith in his aeroplane on the golf links at Datchet on 1st February 1911. He flew over Windsor to visit George V but landed on the golf course, near Moy Lodge in the Slough Road. The excuse was that he had been forced down by a leaking radiator (which was later cured by flattening the leaking pipe with a pair of pliers) but he in fact had lunch with his sister who lived at Moy Lodge!

There are many old buildings in the village, including Church Cottage and Astracot Cottage dating from the 16th century. Cedar House, a 17th century house with a fine cedar tree in the front, had a small powder room where the gentry would   powder their wigs.

Next door there used to be Satis House, occupied for a time by the Astronomer Royal, Dr Herschel, and his sister, but now replaced by a block of flats. The oldest shop is in the High Street and now sells antiques. Formerly it was Gillett's, the butcher's, with its own abattoir and royal coat of arms over the front window. Facing the river is the Post House. Old prints of the bridge show a building here since the 16th century and it could have been a post house where travellers changed horses. Inside is a room said to have been used by Nell Gwynne. The story is that the wife of Charles II refused to live in the same county as 'that woman' so Charles installed Nell in the Post House, just across the river and then in the county of Buckinghamshire.

Datchet House, next to the church, is an 18th century building occupied in the 1930s by Laura La Plant, the film star, who had the whole roof lowered seven inches and her bedroom walls painted with tropical scenes.

Parts of the Manor Hotel (formerly called the 'Horse and Groom') date from the 15th century and the deal panelling in the front bar of the Morning Star is also of the same period. J.K. Jerome in his book *Three Men in a Boat* (1889) mentions that they could not find accommodation at the Manor Hotel or the Royal Stag.

Datchet has a so called Cats' Cemetery. Lady Mabel Cholmondeley, who lived at Leigh House over the turn of the 20th century, had many cats. When they died at least 30 were buried, complete with coffin and tombstone, in an area of shrubbery. When she died in 1928 her will stated that they were not to be disturbed. So when the house was pulled down and the new estate of Leigh Park laid out in the 1930s, the island of shrubs was left in the middle of the road. But all trace of tombstones has gone!

The Beating of the Bounds was first carried out in Datchet in 1634, and was repeated in 1646 and 1655 when stakes showing the boundaries were inspected and repaired. When a boundary mark had been identified or replaced it was the custom for one of the boys in the party to be 'bumped' on the stake whilst being held upside down. This imprinted the position of the boundary on his mind so he could assist in the bumping of the next generation. In 1965 there were great celebrations with a carnival procession and river regatta and ox roasting.

On 30th May 1987 after a blessing by the vicar, the parties set out and eventually linked up at the river front where they were met by the Mayor of Windsor arriving by boat. The carnival procession proceeded to the fete on the recreation ground. The entertainments, with ox roasting, ended with fireworks. On Sunday 31st May a thanksgiving service in St Mary's church was followed by the planting of a commemorative oak by Lord Montagu on the recreation ground.

Donnington

Castles are always places of mystery, and Donnington Castle is no exception. Sir Richard Abberbury received a licence to build a castle at Donnington in 1386. The gatehouse is the only part which now remains standing. The castle has been partly excavated and it is possible to see the outline of the flint walls. Many interesting features, which give an indication to the size and use of the castle, are visible around the walls and gatehouse.

The most eventful days of the castle were during the Civil War, when it was garrisoned for King Charles I and held out in a 20 month siege (31st July 1644 – 1st April 1646). This was the time when most of the destruction took place. During the Second Battle of Newbury, while Sir John Boys defended the castle, King Charles was at nearby Shaw House. On the slopes below the castle are the remains of a 17th century star fort, constructed by Colonel John Boys in 1643-4. In an upstairs room of Shaw House is a plaque encasing a bullet hole, a shot said to have been aimed at the King while he dressed by the window.

In the past workmen have investigated the legend of a

secret tunnel between Donnington Castle and Shaw House. This seems improbable because of the distance between the two buildings and the difference of 140 ft in ground height. No evidence of a tunnel was found, but it is suggested that a hollow space that was found in the southeast corner of the earthworks may have been a secret sally port from which the legend originated. It was from this sally port that the Cavaliers made their famous rush against Dalbier, surprising the Roundheads in their trenches below the castle.

Donnington castle is an interesting place to visit, and much information is available in Newbury Museum. The castle is always open to the public, but cars are not allowed on the drive of Donnington Castle House after 6.30pm.

At Bagnor, on the river Lambourn about one mile upstream from Donnington, is a watermill which dates from 1830. It was used as a corn mill, a fulling mill and a fine paper mill before it was converted into a theatre for its first professional performance in 1967.

In the early days of the theatre, the first seats came from Winchester Cathedral. The lack of insulation rendered the auditorium a much noisier place than it is today. After heavy rain the roar of the mill race provided considerable competition for the actors. On the way to the auditorium from the foyer, the playgoer can still see and hear the waterwheel. There are now 170 seats and the way to the circle and slips is by way of a spiral staircase.

It is a real pleasure to go to a play at the Watermill Theatre on a warm summer evening, spending the interval in the beautiful gardens, watching the trout rise to the mayfly in the river. To make the evening complete, candlelit dinners are served in the 19th century tithe barn restaurant.

Donnington Grove House lies to the west of Donnington village and can be viewed from Grove Road or from the public footpath which leads from Donnington Castle to Bagnor. The house was designed by the architect John Chute and built in 1759. It is three storeys high, castellated and incorporates blue bricks. The front porch rises the whole height of the building. In the late 18th century, the Brummell family bought the house and 'Beau' Brummell, the instigator of Bath 'Society', spent some of his formative years there. A road off Grove Road is named after the family.

Donnington Hospital, a group of almshouses, lies on the west side of Oxford road between Lockets Bridge and Mill Bridge, almost opposite the Priory. Above the gabled entrance is set the arms of Elizabeth I in a garter supported by a dragon and lion. These were made in 1934 by Mr F.C. Thorn of Shaw Hill. The previous coat of arms, which was most likely put in position at the re-foundation of the alms-houses in 1601, was by then very worn and it is now set into the wall of the Hospital porch.

After negotiating the hazards of the notorious Robin Hood roundabout it is with relief that one hurries north-wards towards Shaw or Hermitage. On the east side of this road is Smiths Crescent, houses which are mainly of the Regency period. The houses nos 95, 97 and 99 are probably of the Queen Anne era, but the fronts were rebuilt in Georgian times.

East Garston & Eastbury

Visitors travelling up the Lambourn valley will pass the ancient village of East Garston just off the main road, close to its church and manor house. Continuing their journey through neighbouring Eastbury and arriving at Lambourn, they may wonder why there is no 'West Garston'. The reason is that, like many other villages, East

Garston has had a gradual change of name during its long history.

In the time of King Edward the Confessor, land at East Garston was held by Asgar or Esgar, who gave his name to the settlement and for 200 years it was known as Esgarston or Esegarston.

By the 17th century Estgarston was commonly used and by the 19th century this had become East Garston. This name was adopted by the Post Office and by the Lambourn Valley Railway.

When the inhabitants referred to their native village, they often called it 'Arguson', a name which has been passed on orally until modern times.

In 1904 the vicar of East Garston was Rev John Tudor, whose interest in the history of his parish prompted him to start a campaign to revive the older name of Esgarston. Following a lengthy correspondence in the local press, in which many local historians joined, a petition was sent to the Berkshire County Council by local landowners and signed by many inhabitants, requesting that an order be made under the Local Government Act of 1894 confirming the name to be East Garston.

A well attended public meeting was held at the school, presided over by Mr J.H. Spackman, the Parish Council Chairman. After some discussion during which it emerged that the vicar was almost alone in advocating a return to the older name, an overwhelming majority voted for the village to be called East Garston, the name to which everyone had become accustomed .

East Garston's neighbour, Eastbury, might also be expected to have a western counterpart, but her nearest westerly neighbours are Lambourn, Upper Lambourn and the Wiltshire village of Baydon.

The Westburys, an old local family, owned land and farmed in Upper Lambourn for centuries, but although the hamlet's name has evolved from Uplamborne to the modern version, there is no evidence that this family ever gave their name to their native place.

John Estbury, who founded the Isbury Almshouses in Lambourn in 1502, was the last of a family long associated with Eastbury. His ancestor who died in 1372 was known as John de Estbury. He acquired land in Eastbury which appears to have remained in the possession of the family until the end of the 15th century.

Although Eastbury is undoubtedly the more modern version of Estbury, the almshouses founded by John Estbury were already known as Isbury's almshouses in the early 19th century and this is the official name of them today. Perhaps this is a case where the local pronunciation has been preserved and it may be that one day we will find that Isbury is the name which pre-dates even the 14th century de Estburys.

East Ilsley

East Ilsley, high on the Berkshire Downs, is well known today for the training of racehorses. However, in the past, the village was associated more with sheep than horses.

Berkshire used to be one of the best counties for sheep-rearing. Many of the old churches were built by successful wool merchants in the 14th and 15th centuries. East Ilsley held regular sheep markets, second in size only to Smithfield, with sheep in pens on either side of the village street. A commemoration stone marks the site and since 1975 there has been an annual sheep fair wtih demonstrations of sheep-shearing and related crafts.

Eton Wick

It is surprising how many features of Eton Wick owe their existence to one man, Mr Edward Littleton Vaughan, affectionately known as 'Toddy', a housemaster at Eton College who for more than half a century was a great friend and benefactor to the village.

In 1906 he had built and presented to the village its own village hall, a solidly constructed two-storey red brick building that was the envy of all the surrounding villages at that time. In 1930 he persuaded the County Library to open a branch in the village hall, where it remains to this day. An oak sapling planted by him on the common in Queen Victoria's Jubilee Year 1897 is now a handsome tree, and a small close of council houses built in the 1930s bears his name, Vaughan Gardens. When he died in 1940 a plaque was erected to his memory in the village hall, and at the bequest of his widow who died in 1951 a stained glass window above the altar in the village church commemorates his life and work.

But as well as these outward signs of his generosity, many village activities thrived and still thrive as a result of his encouragement and help. He was an active manager of the village school, president of the football and cricket clubs, supported the horticultural society which held its annual show in his paddock at Wheatbutts, and took the chief part in the formation of the Scout troop and Girl Guides. And indeed the formation of the Eton Wick & Boveney Women's Institute in 1933 was largely through his encouragement and his wife was its first President.

An intriguing piece of Eton history can be seen on the towpath of the Thames just east of Eton Wick.

In 1917 Eton College boy John Lionel Baker was killed in a flying accident at Lincoln. In his memory, knowing his great love of swimming in the Thames, his father Hiatt C.

Baker, a furnisher and draper of Bristol as well as a well known botanist in that area, bought the land at the college swimming place called 'Athens' and presented it to the College. A memorial tablet to John Lionel was erected in the side of the diving mound, called 'The Acropolis'. This tablet was removed when the diving area was discontinued in the 1950s.

In March 1989, following restoration of the towpath by the Thames Heritage Trust, a ceremony was held at 'Athens' restoring the tablet to its original site, together with a commemorative plaque and a seat. At the ceremony was Mr David Baker, the brother of the dead John, who had been traced by Eton Wick & Boveney WI member Kathleen Ware. She had become interested in the story through an odd coincidence, as her first job in Bristol in the 1920s had been as secretary to a Hiatt C. Baker. From college records she found that a Mr E. Baker of Bristol was an Old Etonian and on contacting him was able to confirm that his father

The village hall at Eton Wick

Hiatt C. Baker was the father of John Lionel and also her former employer.

Following aerial photographs which showed a possible causewayed enclosure situated on the north bank of the Thames at Eton Wick, a team of graduates sponsored by the County Council and the Manpower Services Commission excavated a first trial trench in 1984. A ditch segment was located and over 200 pieces of flint and 1,000 sherds of pottery recovered, suggesting the existence of a substantial Bronze Age settlement on the site. In 1985 three further trenches were excavated and pottery recovered. Four areas of Bronze Age and Iron Age activity were located and one trench produced Neolithic flintwork, pottery and bone including an antler comb. Unfortunately further excavation had to be abandoned through lack of funds.

Fawley

This little village in the North Wessex Downs has become a place of pilgrimage for people from all over the world because of 'the Hardy connection'. The great Wessex writer Thomas Hardy's grandmother, Mary Hardy, was probably born at Fawley in 1772. What is certain is that she was an orphan and that she lived for the first 13 years of her life with her aunt in Fawley. Her memories of those years were so painful that she never wished to speak of them in later times.

Perhaps this much-loved grandmother's sad memories coloured Hardy's own view of Fawley and the surrounding countryside, for he chose it as the main setting for one of his latest and most tragic novels, *Jude the Obscure*, not because he found it an enchanting spot, as so many others have, but because the village, which he called Marygreen, and its surroundings struck him as a suitably gloomy place for the ill-fated character Jude Fawley. It has been suggested by some authorities that there is much of Hardy himself in the character of Jude, and that Sue Bridehead is modelled on his cousin Tryphena. Whether this is true or not, at the time he was making notes for the book he wrote to his friend Edmund Gosse that Sue Bridehead was a 'type of woman which has always had an attraction for me'.

Hardy's sister Mary, while teaching at Denchworth, visited the village in 1864 to see if she could trace any of their grand-mother's relations. A year or so later, hearing that the old church, where some of his ancestors were buried, was to be pulled down, Hardy visited the village himself and made a sketch of the church. His journal records his gloomy response to the place: 'I entered', he wrote, 'a ploughed field which might have been called the Valley of Brown Melancholy, where the silence was re-markable.' Although the old church has long since gone, the churchyard is still in existence, albeit in a neglected state.

The little school too, where Sue worked with her hated husband Philotson, still stands.

Jude described the new church of St Mary as 'of modern Gothic design, unfamiliar to English eyes', and Pevsner concurs when he calls it a 'serious, almost forbidding church'. It was built in 1866 by G.E. Street, and one of the stained glass windows is by William Morris.

From Fawley you can follow Jude's route towards Oxford, or 'Christminster' as Hardy calls it, up and across the ancient Ridgeway.

Finchampstead

➤ Before 1854, Longwater Lane was the only road from Finchampstead village to Eversley Green, the present cricket pitch. It passed the Greyhound public house and the end of Fleet Wood to the river Blackwater, then it continued up the bed of the river, which here was called the Longwater, for about 500 yards, to where the present Finchampstead bridge now crosses the river.

Part way down the lane, at Little Green, where four public footpaths converge, a plaque and signpost was erected in 1978 to commemorate the occasion on 6th November 1501, when Henry VII, while hunting in the nearby woods with his sons, Prince Arthur and Prince Henry, was told by the Spanish envoy that the Infanta, Katherine of Aragon had safely reached Dogmersfield. The sign is made out of the wood of an old yew tree, which used to stand on the site, and near some now demolished almshouses.

In the lower level graveyard of St James' church, is a circular unmarked grave. It is eight feet in diameter, grassed in the middle and edged with kerbstones and for many years has been somewhat of a mystery. There is a similar circular grave, but larger, at Bearwood, dedicated to Arthur Frazer and Henrietta Maria Walter. Recent investigations by the local graveyard historian have revealed that a baby, Antony Walter, son of Arthur Frazer and Henrietta Maria, died aged seven months while they still lived in Finchampstead. This is the probable answer to the mystery.

To the right, on the wall between the pews, as you enter through the north door of St James' church, is a poignant reminder of the First World War. This is a Flanders Cross, dedicated to the memory of Lt E.A.F. Corfield, who was killed in 1917. The church itself is mainly Norman, with an

50

18th century brick tower. It stands on an ancient earthwork, enclosed by a bank.

An unusual listed 'building', Grade III, is a length of wall from the end of the present St James' church car park, to the entrance of the manor house. It was built in the 17th century and is the only remains of the former East Court Manor, which was originally near the church.

The Roman influence is evident throughout Finchampstead. The Devil's Highway, a Roman road from Silchester to Staines, crosses into the parish just north of Bulloways Farm, through West Court and on to Simon's Wood, past Heath Pool. The Romans constructed an embankment across a small stream to make this lake. In those days it was a welcome watering place for travellers and now it is enjoyed by the many visitors to this National Trust property.

Commemoration signpost at Finchampstead

Grazeley

The two lanes met at Pound Green: Kybes Lane delighted us with cowslips, but Pump Lane always found our young feet skipping along it, to experience the excitement of pumping the handle of the Pound Green Pump, and finding clear cool water coming out of the spout.

It was probably not such a pleasure to the ladies who had to carry buckets on yokes across their shoulders, back to the Railway Cottages at least a third of a mile away. The farmer from the little farm across the road at least had a hand-drawn water tank to take water to his cattle and cool the milk.

Beside the pump was a commemorative stone which read:

> This land and well with the
> fences surrounding were given by
> the late Dr Robert Wright
> of Grazeley Lodge
> to the inhabitants of the
> ecclesiastical district of Grazeley
> to be held in trust for them by the
> incumbent, churchwardens and
> overseers for the time being.

Now, alas, it has all fallen into ruins, and most people will pass along the lane without even noticing the mound in the hedge, covered by ivy and brambles. Only the brickwork remains, the pump and the inscription having long since disappeared.

However, the owner of Grazeley Lodge, now Grazeley Court Farm, rescued the stone and built it into an old brick wall near the gate. It is there for you to see, if you would like to.

Hampstead Norreys & Peasemore

➤ Staddle stones, more commonly seen today as garden ornaments, were originally used to support the base of barns. This left a gap between the floor of the barn and the ground, and so prevented rats getting into the store. There are still some examples left in the Hampstead Norreys area.

In this area, flints to today's farmer mean constant repairs to tractor tyres. On the other hand, they are put to good use in wall building. In Hampstead Norreys there are not only walls of long standing, but also recently erected garden walls built in the old tradition of brick and flint.

In 1983 an unusual storage cupboard was discovered in the village by people working on their old cottage. It was a sunken, brick-lined room with a domed roof, the entrance to which was in the side of a hill outside their back door. On one wall was a small alcove. A similar room had been found in the village some time earlier, so such storage 'larders' must have been fairly common at one time. They may have been used as cool-houses to store meat and game, or alternatively might have been smoke-houses in the days when many people smoked their own meat. An old village legend of an underground tunnel to Compton might have developed from a sighting of one of these buried storehouses.

In the churchyard is a most unusual monument, erected in 1855 to commemorate the lord of the manor, Job Lowsley. He was so popular with his tenant farmers and their workers, that when he died they collected together all the old iron farm implements they could find and sent the lot off to Bucklebury foundry to be melted down and recast into a huge monument. It has seven steps or tiers, which have since been used to commemorate other members of the Lowsley family, and is surmounted by an iron spire. It is a unique memorial to a much loved squire.

The 'Lucky Hole' in Peasemore can be found in the old flint wall which shields Peasemore House from the road. It has been known and enjoyed by the local children for almost a century and maybe before.

A coin or some other small item is often found inside, so it is usual to replace anything taken out. A button, pin, nut or even a wild flower will do. Sometimes quite a valuable gift can be found, if someone generous and kind has passed that way.

Hare Hatch

Hare Hatch, not far from Wargrave on the Thames, has changed greatly since the 1920s. One villager remembers –

'My brother and I arrived, with our parents, to live at the Horse and Groom, Hare Hatch in 1924. We arrived from London so it was all so different and exciting to be in the country. First of all we had to walk a mile and a half to school. I was eight and my brother six so it seemed a long way. There were no school dinners, so we took sandwiches and a flask of soup. It was a very cold winter and we were frozen by the time we arrived. A boy called Freddie Salt always had two hot baked potatoes in his pockets to keep his hands warm. The school seemed dark with small windows. The headmaster was Mr Quartermain, very strict and fair. I collected birds' eggs and I gave George Webb a halfpenny to climb to the top of the school roof to collect a swift's egg.

'At Christmas, the Mummers came to the Horse and Groom to do their plays, all dressed up in colourful clothes. The old local men told of the days when the Mail coaches stopped on their way to Reading, also there was talk of the distilling of lavender in the area. We also had a quoits alley.

'We had a Mission Hall by the side of the Horse and Groom just in Milly Lane. There was a lay preacher, Mr Chenery, and on Sundays a busy school with coloured texts and annual prizes.

'The Garth Hunt met outside the pub and my father handed out glasses of cherry brandy to the pink-coated huntsmen. One day the hungry hounds rushed into the bar and ate the meat pies which were on display.

'We loved the Berkshire accents! 'Summat' for something; 'a boy chap', a youth; to 'swallow', quilt; a 'cow gown', a smock; 'huck up' to dig up; 'shoy hoy', a scarecrow. The remedy suggested when I had a tiresome cough was goose grease and turpentine!

'I remember the names of various of our customers - Charlie Pocket, Harry House, Sid Prater, Charlie Miles, all agricultural workers, locally. I can still remember the pungent smell of their clothes, especially in winter when they were wet. They sat around an enormous coal fire warming themselves, smoking churchwarden pipes (long clay pipes about twelve inches long and very fragile so they were kept in a rack in the smoke room). There were spittoons on the floor filled with sawdust, much to my father's dismay and he soon did away with them, so some of them used the fire instead, they were quite adept in shooting straight and the coals hissed with the spray! They played shove halfpenny, dominoes, crib and many card games by the hour. Special entertainment was singing, everyone had his own song and someone thumped the piano; Old Gramp Salt's speciality was *To be a farmer's boy*, I swear there were 50 verses to endure.

'We all had fun, worked very hard and enjoyed the different seasons with their festivities'.

Holyport

▰ There are only 17 Real Tennis courts in use in the country today and one of them is in Holyport, having been renovated in 1986 after many years of disuse.

The court originally belonged to The Lodge on Holyport Green and was built in 1889 for Mr Sam Heilbut by a specialist builder, Joseph Bickley, for the sum of £12,000.

Real Tennis, the predecessor of lawn tennis, originated in the 13th century. Henry VIII became very enthusiastic about the game and had a luxury court built at Hampton Court which is still in existence. The rackets used are not quite the same as modern lawn tennis ones and the balls are handmade with needle and thread by each club for their own use.

No-one would guess, watching the intent anglers by the ponds in Stud Green, Holyport, that once this had been the scene of a busy brick-making concern. Clay was dug out where the ponds are and a kiln stood where a cottage called Pondlands now stands .

Just before the First World War the clay pits suddenly flooded, literally overnight, and brick making came to an abrupt halt. The bricks themselves were very individual and marked 'Holyport Brick and Tile Company'. Some are still in existence; two at least have been incorporated into walls with the lettering proudly dislayed.

The original Philberds (named after its owner Roger de St Phylybert) was mentioned in county records of 1208 and was sold in 1248 for £12 16s 4d. The manor of Phylyberts was bought by King Edward in 1352 and the Dean of St George's Chapel, Windsor became its ex-officio guardian until the Commonwealth, when it was sold to raise funds for Cromwell.

The old house was pulled down circa 1780, and a new one built on the same site by a Mr Fuller. This was a large square mansion with turrets! The inside was more attractive with elegant staircases and ceilings, and fireplaces by Adam.

Between 1854 and 1879 it was turned into Philberds School by the Rev Edward Price, whose son Edward later made it into a military academy numbering Winston Churchill and Field Marshal Lord Slim among its pupils.

During the First World War, Philberds was commandeered as a POW camp for 600 German officers, who left it in such a sorry condition that the owner, Major Martineau, decided in 1919 that it was only fit for demolition.

At the present time there is still a 'Philberds' - a tall white house which looks, from the bridge over the M4, as if it stands isolated in the middle of a field, shielded only by a screen of conifers.

Lynden manor is a beautiful house near to Holyport Green and was once known as Hendons Manor. Before the Second World War it was inhabited by the Marquis of Milford Haven and his family, who were connected to the Mountbattens.

Young Philip Mountbatten spent most of his holidays there and after the war, of course, this young man married Princess Elizabeth, now our Queen, and his cousin David Milford Haven was his best man.

Running through the rooms of the manor was the longest model railway in the country, being a complete and detailed replica of the Great Western Railway.

Opposite Hendons Manor were some riding stables, and it was there, under Miss Sybil Smith and her father, that the young Princesses, Elizabeth and Margaret Rose, perfected their horse riding skills. No mention has ever been made of Princess Elizabeth and her future husband meeting at that time, but it is intriguing to wonder. Miss Smith is still living in the village and, up to recent times, was still acting as judge at horse shows.

On the first Saturday in June every year Holyport residents awake to find the Green transformed overnight as if by magic. Marquees have sprouted like huge mushrooms and a large brightly coloured merry-go-round dominates the scene. By mid-morning stalls have been erected and filled with pottery, bric-a-brac, plants, craft work, cakes, books - anything to tempt the customers.

Hoop-la, shove halfpenny, bowling for the pig, all have eager contestants for colourful prizes when the fair opens at 2pm. A queue forms for the Grand Draw tickets in the same tent as the WI stall and the bottle tombola. Vintage cars line up for inspection and brawny tug-of-war teams 'take the strain' with much grunting and shouting, cheered on by spectators. A trailer full of children wheels gently round the green, drawn sometimes by a pair of shire horses and sometimes by a farm tractor. The whole scene is enlivened by the jingly tunes of the merry-go-round until it is silenced for the Master of Ceremonies to announce the names of Miss Holyport and Miss Junior Holyport, and other prize winners.

Then comes the famous Beer Race. Fit and energetic young men set off from the Belgian Arms after downing a half pint of beer, running from pub to pub (half a pint to be swallowed at each one) and back to the finish outside the Lodge.

By mid-morning the next day the green is back to normal till next June.

Hungerford

Hungerford is an attractive town, retaining many of its historic buildings, on the southern slopes of the Kennet valley. It has always in the past depended for its prosperity on the road, canal and rail routes that pass through here, though a sigh of relief greeted the opening of the M4, which bypassed Hungerford and alleviated the huge traffic jams which used to build up in its streets.

Hungerford was on the Bath Road and many of its old inns can trace their history back to coaching days. Coaching may look picturesque to our eyes today but it could be an extremely uncomfortable, if not downright dangerous, way to travel. An anonymous poet in 1717 wrote of *A Journey to Bath and Bristol*, on the route through 'marshy Hungerford that's famed for Beer':

> 'From Hungerford we swift went o'er the
>   Plain,
> Too soon we came to the destructive Lane,
> O fatal way! Here Rocks and craggy Stones
> Our Limbs distorted, and unlock't our Bones,
> The long worn Axle to the Coach, alack!
> Gave here a dismal, unexpected crack.'

One of the greatest of Hungerford's old inns is the Bear. It may date from as far back as the 13th century, but it is definitely shown in records of the 15th century. When it was part of the manor of Chilton Foliat, it was gifted by Henry VIII to five of his six wives in turn. In 1607 it was the property of Sir John Popham, and the arms of the Leybourne-Pophams were incorporated in the sign over the main door.

On Friday 7th December 1688, William of Orange arrived at the Bear just before dark, and over the next two days events took place which changed the course of our national history.

William met representatives of his royal father-in-law, James II. The envoys were the Lords Halifax, Nottingham and Godolphin and they brought a letter from the king.

William was accompanied by a large army and hundreds of irregular cavalry and these together with his royal servants must have placed a great strain on Hungerford. William himself had a bedroom at the Bear and the use of the 'great room', now today's dining room, which is very little changed in the past 300 years.

The envoys were received in William's bedroom, also still virtually unchanged, and he showed great emotion and requested the Lords and gentlemen to consult together, unrestrained by his presence, as to the answer to be given to the letter from James II. This meeting took place in the dining room, a lively meeting of English Lords and William's followers with Lord Oxford in the chair. Passionate argument raged and eventually on Monday 10th December proposals were formulated that all parties could agree to.

This meeting at the Bear Inn resulted in the flight of James II to France and the end of the House of Stuart.

On 7th December 1989 the Tercentenary of Willam and Mary's coronation was commemorated by the unveiling of a plaque outside the hotel, the performance of a community play in the parish church and the presentation to the Bear Hotel of a beautiful tapestry now hung in the reception area, worked by the members of Hungerford Women's Institute.

The coaching trade collapsed in the 1840s and 1850s with the coming of the railway. The railway also caused the demise of Hungerford's other major route of communication and trade, the Kennet and Avon Canal. The canal at Hungerford was opened in 1798, though the full waterway between Bath and Reading was not completed till 1810.

St Lawrence's church, built in 1816, is a reminder of those early days of water-borne trade. It is built of Bath stone, which had never before been used in the town and was only available then because the canal had made it possible to transport heavy goods such as stone long distances for a reasonable price. The old 13th century church had become so dilapidated that it was demolished, and a completely new building was raised.

The canal too effectively died in the 1850s, and Hungerford never again saw the kind of prosperity that it and coaching had brought. The canal itself became neglected and overgrown. During the Second World War it briefly regained importance, as a line of defence against possible invasion, and some of the pillboxes built along it in those days can still be found. However, it took the increased interest in leisure activities and in the working past to bring the canal back to life, and it was reopened along this section in 1974.

Hurley

On 24th May 1989 a new bridge was opened over the Thames at Hurley, visible only from the river, the footpath and a few nearby houses. Temple Footbridge provides a link in the continuous riverside footpath between Henley and Marlow, and is on the site of the old Temple ferry which closed in 1953. The project was instigated by Thames Water, who received practical assistance from Buckinghamshire County Council and contributions from Berkshire County Council, the Royal Borough of Windsor and Maidenhead, Hurley Parish Council and the Ramblers Association.

Hurley itself is an ancient settlement, its present church of St Mary the Virgin created from the nave of the old priory church. There has probably been a church or chapel on this spot since the 7th century, and in 1086 it became a cell of the Benedictine Abbey of Westminster. The priory was dissolved by Henry VIII in 1536, but some remains can

Temple Footbridge, Hurley

still be found - the tithe barn (which is now a private house), the dovecote, and the outlines of the cloisters and dormitories.

The Lovelace Memorial in the sanctuary of the church commemorates a colourful local family. It is an amalgam of two striking memorials - the two figures who look at first glance as if they are kneeling have in fact lost their

lower halves. The Lovelace family bought the manor in 1545 and built Ladye Place, named in deference to the Virgin Mary. Richard Lovelace sailed with Sir Francis Drake and made his fortune from raiding Spanish galleons. He was created Lord Lovelace of Hurley in 1627.

The third Lord Lovelace, John, was heavily involved in the Rye House Plot in 1683 to kidnap and perhaps assassinate Charles II at Rye House in Hertfordshire. John was a committed Whig and his party had come to believe that Charles intended to bring back the Roman Catholic religion. At one point England had seemed almost on the point of civil war over the issue, so highly did tempers run. Although the leaders of the Plot were executed and others were imprisoned, John Lovelace was soon back at Ladye Place, plotting.

Ladye Place had been built over the burial crypt of the priory, and it was in those cold vaults that he and his fellow conspirators met. After the accession of the Catholic James II, John was imprisoned, but in 1688 William of Orange and Mary accepted the throne and John was once again in favour. William made him Captain of the Gentlemen Pensioners in gratitude.

Ladye Place was demolished in 1837, although its crypt, where the Glorious Revolution was planned, still exists.

Hurst

About a mile from the attractive village of Hurst is the house called Haines Hill, the oldest parts of which date back to the early 1600s. A local man, Bert Yde, went to work there as a gardener's boy after he left school. After serving in the First World War, he came back to Haines Hill and bought a few acres of agricultural land from the estate so that he could set up his own business.

His daughter recalls that when the Second World War was declared, as his war effort, he 'took on the kitchen garden where he had worked as a boy, at the great rent of £20 pa. Would it pay? It did of course, and I enjoyed many happy hours there. Not only in the twelve ft walled garden but also in a wild orchard beyond, where wood anemones, primroses, violets and more grew. A truly fairy-tale place.

'Inside the garden, the walls were covered with all types of fruit trees. Peach and nectarine houses were on the south side, where a lovely chimonanthus grew. There were two vineries, one even had English muscats, the best grapes of all, as well as raspberries, strawberries, currants, figs and asparagus beds. Most of our beehives were installed there, to pollinate the blossom. Two pigs, in the far corner, one for the Ministry and one for us. Each time they were due for slaughter the local butcher had the head for brawn and my mother had to deal with the rest without the aid of a fridge or deep freeze. A job she did not look forward to! On the north outside wall was a mushroom shed and inside another apple and pear cold store.

'To look after this, two land army girls were employed. As much food as possible was produced, but not tomatoes, they were grown at home together with lettuce and radish etc.'

Such kitchen gardens, which produced enough food to feed the large household of family and servants at the 'big house' have all but disappeared today, the land sold and developed or allowed to run to wilderness, its original purpose forgotten.

Inkpen

The village of Inkpen in the south-west corner of Berkshire contains one of the few remaining sites in the United Kingdom where the wild crocus (*Crocus Vernus*) continues to bloom in profusion. Called Crocus Field, it in fact covers two meadows separated by a hedgerow and stream, totalling just over seven acres. The northern meadow where the population of crocuses is most concentrated in spring is also rich in herbs and grasses while the south meadow is dominated by rushes with fewer flowering plants. The land offers poor grazing and so is a rare site of unimproved pasture which, in time past, has been used as a source of clay for local potteries, the last of which closed in 1920.

Local tradition asserts that the crocuses were introduced to Inkpen from southern Europe by the Knights Templar – a survey of 1185 records that the Knights were given land at Templeton just north of Inkpen. An alternative and more likely theory is that they came to these fields as garden escapes, possibly during the 18th century when several of the large houses in the area had gardens designed and created, entailing the removal and dumping of large amounts of garden soil and debris on surrounding land.

With the aid of grants from the Nature Conservancy Council, the World Wildlife Fund, Newbury and Inkpen councils and several concerned individuals, the Berks, Bucks and Oxfordshire Naturalists' Trust purchased the site in May 1986. It is now protected and maintained as a permanent nature reserve of special scientific interest and attracts visitors from all parts of the country.

Wild crocuses at Inkpen

Knowl Hill

One of the biggest Steam Rallies in the south of England now takes place here annually in August. The village hall and adjoining car park were built from the proceeds of the first few events, as was intended; a new doctors' sugery came later – prior to this the doctor came from Wargrave twice a week to administer medicines in the small back room of the Seven Stars hostelry! These are now well established and a Trust Fund for monies accumulated over the intervening years is being used to help local deserving causes and organisations.

In the Queen's Jubilee year, 1977, Dutch elm disease destroyed the elms on the hill, called the Clumps, and the whole area had to be cleared, re-seeded, landscaped and replanted. This was funded by the Rally and now a variety of young trees are thriving on the knoll for the pleasure of generations to come.

An old inhabitant told how in the late Victorian years the young girls of the village would walk and have picnics on the knoll. In those days the vicar and his wife were very important people, on a par with the gentry, and the vicarage was close by, so that when the vicar's wife appeared suddenly they would quickly scurry into the bushes on the common to avoid having to curtsy to her, which was expected of them.

The family brick and tile business, founded over 100 years ago, has now become part of a larger complex of companies, keeping up with progress, but a few years ago arc lights and cameras could be seen, and weird noises emitted from the workings when the location was used as a background for the films *The Land That Time Forgot* and *Journey to the Centre of the Earth*.

The Seven Stars public house, dating from the late 1600s, stands back in a lay-by with a small green separating it from the speeding traffic of the A4. Once known as the Buccleigh Arms, as it was owned by the Earl of Buccleigh, it was later renamed the Seven Stars (his heraldic symbol), and in more recent years the adjoining old coach house building became an auction room for antiques. Lately it has been restored and updated to an attractive eating place, incorporating a bowling alley, which is very popular.

The green was notorious in the 1800s for being the venue for prize fighting, and hordes of people would rush down from London to witness the contests. The local Magistracy was taken to task in the *Berkshire Chronicle* in January 1843 for allowing the 'disgusting scenes to take place'. It is said that several highwaymen met their Maker on a gibbet near the Seven Stars!

Before the Second World War the Mummers were to be seen regularly at Christmas time at Knowl Hill performing their play, accompanied by a melodian, and by their collections raised sufficient money to buy the first piano for the old village hall, an Army camp building obtained from Arborfield.

Knowl Hill garage to the west of the village is thought to have been the site of a smithy which served the coaches which travelled the Bath Road. It is still very prominent in the life of the people round and about and has been greatly extended in recent years. The late Mr John Fidler, son of the original owner, was very interested in the preservation of old things and when the old Town Hall in Maidenhead was demolished for a rebuilding programme, he obtained the old clock. The mechanism is now mounted in the window of the showroom where it can be seen still working today, and the clock face is fitted to the facade of the garage, keeping very good time.

Lambourn

◣ In the centre of the village of Lambourn stand two famous landmarks — the ancient church of St Michael and All Angels and the almshouses of John Isbury. Between the two there is a narrow footpath known as Three Post Lane, which joins the Market Place with the Upper Lambourn Road near the Royal British Legion Club.

The numerous pedestrians who use this route daily may have noticed two doorways. One at the Upper Lambourn end was the entrance to the Hippisley School. The school was founded in 1753 when Organ Hippisley,a member of the family who then lived in Lambourn Place, left £3 a year to pay a school-master to teach six boys. Later members of the Hippisley family added to the salary and built the school, thus enabling a larger number of boys to be taught on weekdays and on Sundays. The school was discontinued when the Church schools were built in the High Street in 1852, but the Organ Hippisley Charity continues as part of the Lambourn United Charities and the money is still paid annually to the headmaster. The building was demolished and the date over the door was destroyed when the modern housing estate was built in Lambourn Place grounds.

The second doorway now leads to the housing estate, but formerly had a heavy oak door which was the entrance to Lambourn Place, by which the residents came to and from church. The doorway is surmounted by the arms of the Essex family who lived in the house in the 16th and 17th centuries.The date over the doorway, 1603, was during the time of Sir William Essex. The tomb of his great grandfather, Sir Thomas Essex can still be seen in St Katherine's Chapel in the church. Sir William was the patron of the poet Joshua Sylvester.

Sylvester was a well known poet in his day, but out of

two large volumes of verse, only the fragments which mention Lambourn are remembered. One of these fragments describes the strange phenomenon of the river Lambourn, which is dry in part of the winter and unlike many small streams, runs through the summer.

The river still dries up from September until late January, although the pattern has never been quite regular. In some years there is water right through the winter and sometimes the river bed has been dry for 18 months. It can be observed that the flow is related to the rainfall on the downs two or three months earlier, but predictions are often wildly inaccurate. When the 'springs' are high the river extends from its main source in Lynch Wood right through the village of Upper Lambourn, and another small stream rises near Seven Barrows flowing via North Farm and the new housing estates near Mill Lane into the main river.

Since modern pumping has lowered the levels, water no longer rises in Windsor House paddock. Formerly a small lake appeared which drained through the old Lambourn Garages site and the middle of the village into the river near Oxford Street bridge. This has not occurred for more than 30 years, but who will say it can never happen again?

In Baydon Road can still be seen the Old Pest House, now a carefully restored cottage but originally the place to which the victims of smallpox and other infectious diseases were sent.

In 1754 the parishioners of Lambourn petitioned the Earl of Craven for a piece of land to build a pest house. The Earl, who as lord of the manor owned all uncultivated land, willingly granted the request and the work was started.

The overseers raised the money by borrowing on the capital of Christina Organ's Charity. They undertook to make the payments to the poor from the poor rate. A record still exists of the payments made for labour and materials. By the mid 19th century the building was no longer used for its intended purpose and it was eventually sold as two cottages. The money borrowed from the charity was then returned and Christina Organ's bequest made in 1633 still forms part of the Lambourn United Charities.

Lambourn Memorial Hall in Oxford Street is the meeting place of Lambourn WI and several other village organisations. Built in the 1970s, it is the second hall on the site, but before this the site was occupied by two old cottages, one of which was the birthplace of George Clement Martin, said to be the only Lambourn man to become nationally famous. As organist of St Paul's Cathedral he was knighted by Queen Victoria for composing music for the thanksgiving service at her Diamond Jubilee in 1897.

Born in 1844, George Martin was first introduced to music in the Lambourn Brass Band and was a teenager when the Willis organ was first installed in Lambourn church. He learned to play this organ and came to the notice of Sir John Stainer, who gave him music lessons at Oxford enabling him to get a degree in music at that university.

After a period as organist at Lambourn and in Edinburgh he became Stainer's assistant at St Paul's and succeeded him as organist and choirmaster. There is a plaque on the front of the Memorial Hall and another in the parish church commemorating George Martin's life and recording his connection with Lambourn.

Langley Marish

► Whilst speeding along the A4 Bath Road towards Heathrow airport, spare a passing thought for the eastern edge of the town John Betjeman loved to hate – Slough.

Langley Marish was once a long narrow parish quite separate from Slough and, at its southernmost end, contained three villages: Middle Green, George Green and Horsemoor Green.

The Enclosure Act of 1809 changed the face of the parish, as the three main greens, along with other smaller greens, were lost as common grazing to the village folk. All that remains today are the names of these greens, still in use, and among the large housing estates many roads named for people prominent in the history of the area.

But the most interesting part of the parish today centres around a peaceful oasis in what was once the very small main village. Here is the church, St Mary the Virgin, once a chapel of ease for the church at Wraysbury. Opposite stands the timbered Red Lion public house, and on either side of the church, a row of almshouses. These almshouses were built by Sir John Kedermister and Sir Henry Seymour between 1617 and 1689, and are still in use as dwelling houses today.

The church itself was probably built during the 11th and 12th century, with additions and alterations throughout the years. Its exterior presents pleasing contrasting textures of brick, flint and stone.

The interior contains many varied and interesting features, including a fine Jacobean pulpit and a transept screen made of Coade stone, the artificial substance produced in the 18th century which defeats all modern attempts to reproduce. However, the glory of St Mary's is still well-hidden from sight. On the south side of the church is the Kedermister Pew, entered by its own door from the churchyard.

Occupying the width of the chapel in the south transept, the pew was built in the early 17th century by the then lord of the manor, Sir John Kedermister, for his family's own use. The pew has an eastern appearance with lattice windows through which the family could see the whole of the church and not be seen. Entering the pew, there are pine benches for seating, and on all sides it is richly decorated with the arms of the Kedermisters and biblical texts, and painted on many of the panels is the all-seeing Eye of God. The door leading to the churchyard was the family's private entrance, and another door leads to Sir John's library, which he provided for the benefit of the minister in Langley or any other clergy in Buckinghamshire who might wish to use it.

The whole interior of the room is most sumptuously and colourfully decorated with more than 250 painted panels, and a focal point is the handsome fireplace with elaborate over-mantel displaying the arms of the Kedermister family. The room is lined with book shelves enclosed by panelled doors, and portraits of Sir John and his wife, Lady Mary, are painted on the insides of two of the doors. The 300 or so books are mainly theological works in Latin, the most valuable being the 11th century illuminated Kedermister Gospels which is on indefinite loan to the British Museum.

They include also a 17th century Pharmacopolium, a collection of family remedies compiled by John and Mary Kedermister.

The greatest treasures are too valuable to be kept at the church, and two gilt chairs and an embroidered kneeler are housed at the Victoria and Albert Museum.

Despite lacking these treasures, the library is still a place of great interest and beauty - well worth a detour across the now tarmacadamed long lost greens and villages of the parish of Langley Marish.

Following the death of the last lord of the manor Sir Robert Harvey in 1931, Langley Park estate was acquired by the County Council in 1945 and with it the manorial rights. The chapel, pew and library then became the private property of the County Council, which as lord of the manor has the care of this remarkable family pew and church library.

The chapel, pew and library may be visited by appointment with the Curator. Additionally there are days when it is open to the public at specified times – usually the first Sunday in the months of June to September.

Leckhampstead

◣ This lovely little village is placed high on the Berkshire Downs above the Wantage to Newbury road. It was mentioned in the Domesday Book. The Anglo-Saxon work 'leac' literally means 'a leek', but the term was used in a general sense for garden herbs. 'Leckhampstead' broadly describes a homestead or farm having a kitchen garden.

On a triangular green in the centre of the village is an unusual war memorial comprising an obelisk placed on a plinth. The two clocks positioned on the north and south faces, above the inscriptions of the fallen, have machine-gun bullets denoting minutes, rifle ammunition forming Roman numerals and bayonets for hands. Surrounding the monument are chains taken from a battleship which fought at the battle of Jutland, supported on shell cases.

Hangman Stone Lane may seem a strange name for the road from Chaddleworth to Boxford. But all is revealed when one hears the local story connected with it; for it was in this lane that a local sheep stealer came to an untimely end. Having freshly stolen a sheep from a Chaddleworth farmer, the thief slung his awkward parcel over his shoulders with a rope which he held onto around his neck. Travelling towards Boxford he sat down against a large stone for a rest. He soon fell asleep – but was destined never to wake up. The sheep struggled to get free, and the man was 'hanged' by the cord! His ghost is believed to haunt the lane. The Hangman's Stone, as it is now known, can be found opposite a trackway just before the turning to Leckhampstead, on the boundary of three parishes.

Littlewick Green

At the bottom of the green, Walnut Tree Cottage (circa 1480), sadly now minus the old walnuts but basking in the splendour of a giant yew and tall firs, is the oldest dwelling in Littlewick Green. Mr Richard Hill (1855 - 1939) was a many faceted man and lived for the greater part of his life in this cottage, wherein once lay a mouth-watering sweet shop, displaying in a tiny window much-coveted sherbert dabs, aniseed balls and gob-stoppers of every hue for a halfpenny or a penny each.

Amongst other things he was a well digger of some repute. His wells were not only on home ground but in other villages covering all points of the compass. He left two within the vicinity of his own cottage – one on the village green, constructed for safety purposes into an ornamental well during the 1930s, and the other just outside his home on his own land, which he closed up and has been truly hidden for many a long year. It is now a miniature garden within a garden.

Every Guy Fawkes night, to the delight of the village children, the vicar would light a bonfire which would crackle merrily on the green near to the lychgate. They would roast potatoes on the dying embers and revel in the old custom. It would seem, however, that this did not instil joy into everyone and Richard Hill was asked by two lady residents if, at their expense, he would arrange for a group of trees to be planted encircling the area where the bonfire stood. This he did and for many decades now the village has enjoyed the beauty of this glorious cluster of trees – a mixture of limes, green and copper beeches and white and red horse chestnuts. They are not only a lovely feature of the village but provide shade of which the green is rather bereft and there is a bonus – children can still enjoy this site as a fascinating play area. The hidden factor is in the remains of the old chalk pit which lay below the site where the bonfire brightly burned.

Time, unfortunately, has seen our footpaths, vital ditches and the historic parish pound of White Waltham which was in the Littlewick part of the parish, pass into oblivion. They have vanished behind garden boundaries and are lost for ever. A right of way exists across the green which is a common – cricket has been played on this ground since before the turn of the century but players would always halt the game to allow the housewives, heavily laden with shopping baskets on each arm, to wend their way across the pitch (the shortest route from the bus stop to their respective cottages). Whilst these ladies observed this right it remained so, but as they disappeared so did the right – whilst cricket was in progress.

Miss Bertha Lamb, the founder of Littlewick Green WI in the year of 1918, lived in a house at Littlewick which was rather unusual. Its doors were not exactly open to an uninvited lady by the name of Dorcas Noble, who undeterred, just slipped in through the walls and out again the same way. Her visits were persistent through time and in the 1960s, the residents of that period decided that enough was enough and that identification of both lady and her

Ornamental well outside Walnut Tree Cottage, Littlewick Green

purpose was overdue. The then newly formed Maiden-head Archaeological and Historical Society were called upon for their expertise and were invited to commence on a 'dig' in the grounds around the house which proved fruitful, resulting in finds of various Roman artefacts and human bones. Most importantly, the house itself had been built over the foundations of a Roman dwelling.

Dorcas was apparently a Vestal Virgin from Weycock Hill Temple in Waltham St Lawrence, lying beyond Little-wick's Roman settlement of Black Vere. The site of Bertha Lamb's house lay in the path from the temple which Dorcas Noble regularly trod to keep a love tryst. Unfortu-nately, this priestess forgot to honour her oath of virginity to Vesta when she gave her heart to one of the Nevilles of Billingbear and, not improving matters, she practised witchcraft to win his affections back when he transferred them to another. She had completely let the side down and sadly was beheaded for using sorcery (forbidden by Roman law).

The site of Black Vere is marked, in the midst of farm-land, by a thick, circular forest of trees which vegetate above a fair share of Roman history. Nearby are traces of the Roman road, the Camlet Way connecting Colchester and St Albans with Silchester.

Lower Earley

➤ The massive new development of Lower Earley, begun in the late 1970s, is said to have been the largest new development project in Europe, with between 8,000 and 9,000 houses planned for up to 20,000 new inhabitants. Over the years the area has assumed a new identity as it has been eaten up by the spread of Reading, and you must look closely for traces of days gone by, which were full of history and tradition.

Only the river Loddon flows on, regardless of change. Records show that King John met the great men of the nation at Loddon Bridge to discuss the impoverished state of the nation. In 1779 Loddon Bridge was rebuilt at a cost of £102 18s 0d, and became a toll gate. The land near the river was very marshy and canes made from hazel, hornbeam, ash and sweet chestnut were stripped and the 'rods' sent to London.

The present Sindlesham Mill was built in the 18th century for the use of farmers. The mill is now a bar and restaurant. Sindlesham Farmhouse dates from Georgian times and in later years was a dairy farm as well as an arable farm.

The great houses and estates which once existed at Earley have gone, and the past is hidden beneath houses and roads. Maiden Erlegh estate covered the area roughly between Wilderness Road, Beech Lane and Mill Lane. The mansion was built in the late 19th century on an earlier site, and was owned from 1903 by Solomon 'Solly' Joel, who made many additions, such as a palm court, a marble indoor swimming pool, ornamental gardens and a stud farm. After he died in 1931 the estate was sold and for a time the house was used as a school. In the end it was sold for development, and Solly Joel's mansion was demolished in 1960.

Erleigh Court estate was also sold in the 1930s. It had originally been the medieval manor of Erlegh St Bartholomew, and was owned in the 19th century by Lord and Lady Sidmouth. They donated the site for the Royal Berkshire Hospital in Reading and also the ground for the building of St Peter's church in Earley in 1844. Erleigh Court was demolished in 1935. In 1947 Whiteknights Park estate was acquired for the University of Reading.

There is a charitable success story to come out of the large development of Lower Earley. It goes back into the 1800s when there was an area of land for common use in Earley. Under the Enclosure Acts of the 1800s these areas were absorbed into fields and about twelve acres of land were enclosed for the benefit of the poor of Earley.

In 1903 the Charity Commissioners instigated a scheme whereby trustees were appointed to administer the land. The land was let and the income was used for helping needy cases in the Earley area, continuing over the years up to the present time, until the Lower Earley development commenced. Berkshire County Council then took the option on the land for use as a secondary school site. They reviewed this option in 1987 and the trustees decided to dispose of the land because it was in the middle of the development area. The County Council approved the sale of the land except for two acres, which the trustees retained for their use on a suitable project.

The sale of the land realised just over £6 million, which then had to be invested by the trustees and the income used for the benefit of the poor of Earley.

On the two acres the trustees had retained they decided to commission a residential home for the elderly and the Charity Commissioners gave permission for £2 million of the £6 million to be used for the construction of this particular project. The Trustees deal with applications for cases of need currently referred to them by voluntary bodies and the Social Services and the area covered is within the parish of Earley and the eastern part of Reading Borough.

Other aid is given in forms of grants tied up to two former charities which are now amalgamated — branches of widows and apprenticeship charities. It is possible to give grant aid to certain cases in the educational field, for instance.

Maidenhead

Berkshire is not a county one associates with great megaliths, however there are still a few standing stones to be seen if you know where to look. In the cemetery of St Mark's church in All Saints Avenue, Maidenhead can be seen the last remains of a stone row which once passed through East Berkshire. The single standing stone there formed part of a long avenue of stones in prehistoric times, which would have included the 'Cookham Stone' and 'Tarry Stone' in Cookham village. What were they for? For religious ceremonies, as boundary markers or memorials? We shall probably never know.

In Northumbria Road at Cox Green, Maidenhead there is a plaque which marks the site of one of the oldest pieces of Berkshire history. In times gone by a Roman farmer and his family lived here in their villa. It was not an elaborate complex, but a modest farmstead complete with bath house and granaries. Excavations in 1960 revealed that it dated from the 1st to the 4th centuries.

Maidenhead is therefore an ancient settlement, though for many centuries it was controlled by the then larger and more important parishes of Bray and Cookham. It did not become a parish in its own right until 1870. In the Domesday Book it was recorded as Elentone, and the name Maidenhead appears to date from about 1296, when a new wharf (or 'hythe') was built on the river. Its importance came when the bridge over the Thames brought the main road to and from London through this little hamlet.

During the coaching era Maidenhead saw over 90 coaches a day through its streets. Great coaching inns grew up at this, the first stop on the road from London to the West, the most important perhaps being the Sun, at the bottom of Castle Hill, on the corner of Marlow Road.

The Greyhound in the High Street, which was burned

down in 1735, was host in 1647 to a sad figure, the captive Charles I. He was brought here from Caversham, where he was the prisoner of the Army, and was reunited with his children 'to his infinite content and joy', as Clarendon recorded it.

Another monarch who came to Maidenhead was James I, and there is an amusing story of his encounter with the Vicar of Bray over dinner at the Bear Inn, also in the High Street. James arrived at the inn tired and hungry, having been out hunting. He was alone, as he had become separated from his companions, and the landlord did not recognise him. There was little available to eat, but the vicar and his curate, who were sitting down to their dinner, agreed that the traveller could join them. James, however, carried no money and, having eaten part of the vicar's repast, could not pay his share of the cost. The vicar was most upset, but the curate, who had enjoyed the stranger's company, was happy to help. Then, as in all good stories, the stranger was revealed as the King, when his hunting companions arrived in quest of him at the inn. One can imagine the vicar's mortification, and trepidation! However, the King took no revenge on the vicar, and contented himself with rewarding the kind curate with a post at Windsor.

There are few buildings left of historic Maidenhead, thanks to the town's growth and expansion in the 19th and 20th centuries. The churches are all of the 19th century, except the parish church itself, which was rebuilt in 1964-5. The earlier church of St Andrew and St Mary Magdalene, which may have stood on the site of the original 13th century chapel, was demolished in 1824. It was situated in the centre of the High Street and was blocking the ever-increasing traffic, as well as being too small for the increased population. The new church was built on the present site, the building of the 1820s itself having been demolished.

Maidenhead's finest hour, perhaps, came at the end of the 19th century and the beginning of the 20th. Skindles, built from the old Orkney Arms inn by William Skindle, became the essential place to dine for the playboys and debutantes who came flocking to the 'Jewel of the Thames'. The railway made it easy to reach Maidenhead, and the river became the   fashionable place to display wealth and privilege, enjoyed no less by the trippers who came to watch the rich at play. The town got itself quite a risqué reputation, and there was a famous little quip - 'Are you married or do you live in Maidenhead?' Apparently, when the site of the Brigade of Guards Club was excavated by the local archaeological society, gold wedding rings were common finds in the Victorian rubbish pits, thrown away by young ladies before they returned to their respectable homes from a weekend in Maidenhead!

Mortimer (Stratfield Mortimer)

Present-day Mortimer is mostly 19th and 20th century, but memories of its long history lie hidden in its street and place names. Its own name originates from the Norman manor belonging to Ralf Mortimer in 1086. Stratfield (Stradfeld) meant 'open land traversed by a Roman road', in this case the Londinium to Calleva road, the Devil's Highway.

Hammonds Heath was probably originally 'Amens Heath', so-called, it is thought, because the parish clerk lived there and had rights on the heath.

Longmoor is a reminder of the settlements on former common land to the west of this road which, with the associated hamlets of Five Oaken and Groves Corner were known in the 17th century, and by 1840 numbered over 30 dwellings. Now practically all have disappeared, and their main thoroughfares are overgrown footpaths.

The Carpenters Arms and Turners Arms are public houses named for two of the wood-working trades arising from the plentiful supplies in the surrounding woods, where evidence of old coppicing may still be seen.

In Kiln Lane is the site of a brick works that was still producing bricks in the 1930s, and many buildings in Mortimer are decorated with the dark ends (headers) of those bricks.

Welshman's Road is a reminder of the Welsh drovers who passed through with their stock on their way to the Mortimer Horse and Welsh Cattle Fairs, in November and May each year. Goodboys Lane is named after a family who held land there in the 16th century, and similarly Butlers Lane remembers Thomas Botiller, a 15th century landowner. Windmill Road was cut near the site of the old windmill in 1805-6.

A new Methodist church has been built in West End Road, but the original chapel is down Drury Lane. It is now a private dwelling, but the old graveyard still remains beside it.

Two Iron Age tumuli are hidden amongst pine trees at the north-west corner of the crossroads at the end of Victoria Road.

A rare Saxon tombstone can be found inside St Mary's church, brearing the inscription:-

'On 8th before Kalends of October Aegalward
son of Kypping was laid in this place. Blessed
be he who prays for his Soul. Toki wrote me.'

Aegalward, the son of the lord of the manor, was an historian, and worked on the Anglo-Saxon Chronicles.

The man who had the stone carved, Toki, was an important and wealthy courtier at the court of King Canute, who ruled England from 1017 to 1035. There are very few of these Saxon stones left after so many centuries have passed.

Driving along the Burghfield to Padworth road, through the wooded plantations of Mortimer Common, it is difficult to imagine the grizzly scene which once confronted travellers at the junction to Ufton. For swinging in the breeze here were the bodies of two young lads clamped in irons. Abraham Tull (aged 19) and William Hawkins (aged 17) robbed and murdered an old labourer, William Billimore, in January 1787, because they had no money to spend at the Reading Fair. They were caught a few days later after selling the old man's watch in Maidenhead. Sentenced to be hanged near the scene of the crime, the two brought a crowd of 10,000 people to this quiet spot, still known as Gibbet Piece.

Newbury

Newbury's prosperity in the Middle Ages was built on the cloth trade. Walking down Northbrook Street in Newbury, many people must pass the former home of the wealthiest clothier in England, without even noticing it. At the junction with little Marsh Lane, a footpath running between shops, stands the timber-framed north end of Jack O'Newbury's House.

John Smallwood, alias John Winchcombe, alias Jack of Newbury, came to Newbury as an apprentice cloth-maker, yet it was not long before he had married his employer's widow and enlarged his new cloth business so that he was able to open the first true factory in the country. It was said to employ nearly 1,000 people and to have had 200 looms at work, and reached from Jack's house to what is now

The Falkland Memorial at Newbury

Victoria Park. Jack was an extremely wealthy and influential figure of the day. He entertained Henry VIII and Catherine of Aragon at his house in Northbrook Street, covering the floor with azure cloth for the occasion. The king was so delighted with his host that he wished to knight him, but Jack begged to be allowed to remain 'a poor clothier' until his dying day. His son John, however, accepted the Bucklebury estate, formerly belonging to Reading Abbey, from Henry in 1540.

Jack can be seen commemorated in a brass in St Nicolas' church, dressed in the fur-edged robe of a merchant. This large church, over 140 ft long, is an expression in stone of the wealth which the cloth trade brought to Newbury in the late Middle Ages. The Norman church was rebuilt in the early 1500s, largely financed by Jack and his son. The west tower is dated 1532 and that appears to have been the final part to be built.

The church was the scene in 1556 of the trial of the Newbury Martyrs. Jocelyn Palmer, a master at Reading grammar school, Thomas Askew and a weaver called John Gwyn were all condemned to death here for heresy in the reign of Mary Tudor, who tried so hard to re-establish the Catholic faith in England. The three men were burned at the stake at the Sandpits by Enborne Road.

Jack of Newbury's place in the cloth trade was to some extent taken by William Dolman, another wealthy merchant, whose son Thomas bought the manor of Shaw and commenced the building of Shaw House in the 1550s. This lovely house is now used as part of a school. There is an odd story behind the mottoes carved on the portico of the house.

Before beginning to build the house, Thomas Dolman retired from his cloth business, which unfortunately coincided with a general decline in the trade itself. The unemployed of Newbury made their feelings known with the somewhat awkward rhyme–

'Lord have mercy upon us sinners!
Thomas Dolman has built a new house and
has turned away all his spinners!'

Thomas must have been deeply angered by the fuss, for he went so far as to have carved in stone on the front of his new house a Greek phrase meaning 'Let no jealous enter', and a rather unpleasant Latin inscription meaning 'The toothless envies the eater's teeth, and the mole despises the eye of the goat'!

In 1811 John Coxeter of Greenham was certain that the new machinery he had had installed in his clothmill could bring back the days of Newbury's pre-eminence in the cloth trade. He was asked by Sir John Throckmorton of Buckland if he could weave a coat in one day, from the back of a sheep to the back of a man in the hours between sunrise and sunset. On Coxeter's assurance that he could, Sir John placed a wager of 1,000 guineas. After a day of frantic activity Sir John won his bet, and sat down to dinner that night in the Pelican inn wearing his Newbury Coat. The coat was shown at the Great Exhibition in 1851, and it is still preserved in the Throckmorton family home at Coughton Court, near Alcester.

Travellers leaving Newbury and heading for Andover through Wash Common may glimpse an impressive memorial column as they drive by. Many people assume it is dedicated to those who fell in the First or Second World Wars but the Falkland Memorial actually commemorates an event much further back in our history.

The first Battle of Newbury (September 1643) was fought around the Wash Common and Enborne Heath area and Lucius Cary, Viscount Falkland, was killed in a cavalry charge near Wash Farm. His sacrifice was not forgotten, however, for in September 1878 the Falkland Memorial was unveiled by the Earl of Carnarvon to commemorate the 6,000 officers and men who had been killed in the battle 235 years before.

Old Windsor

Long before the Windsor of today was even a settlement, Old Windsor was an important Saxon town. William the Conqueror decided to build a new castle of stone outside the old town, leaving the wooden palace to fall into ruins, and today there is no trace of the forerunner of Royal Windsor. Old Windsor dwindled into the attractive village it is today.

The most important building left is the Norman parish church, dedicated – unusually – to two saints: St Peter and St Andrew. It stands by the river on the site of the original Saxon settlement.

Memorials of interest in the church include the recumbent effigy of Sir Charles Augustus Murray, KCB, a colourful Victorian diplomat who presented the first hippopotamus to the London Zoo. Thomas Sandby is commemorated too, who with his more famous brother, Paul, was an early watercolour artist. In the churchyard is the box tomb of Mrs Brinsley Sheridan, wife of the 18th century playwright.

The actress Mary Robinson is also buried here. She was a well known actress of the 18th century, who played Shakespearian roles at Drury Lane, and who became known as 'Perdita' after her role in *The Winter's Tale* that brought her to the notice of the Prince of Wales, later George IV. She became his mistress in 1779 but he eventually tired of her. Although she was given a pension, she supported herself by writing. She died in poverty at the age of 42, in 1800.

Old Windsor Hospital (part of King Edward VII Hospital) is a fine Victorian building, which was built as the workhouse to serve several parishes, and was thus known as 'The Union'. It has an attractive chapel and, in addition to the main building, once used as Part III accommodation but now largely disused, there is a laundry building which, in the 1960s was the Maternity Department: many local children were born there.

There is also a range of 'temporary' huts which are now the wards and ancillary buildings. The hospital now caters only for old people.

One interesting relic of its workhouse days can be seen in an outbuilding which has small holes in the walls. Apparently, workhouse inmates were set to the task of breaking up stones, and the resulting pieces, used presumably for road mending, had to be small enough to pass through these holes.

Pangbourne

▬ There is a delightful Victorian Pump House well hidden in the outskirts of Pangbourne, but amazingly near to the M4 motorway. It was built by Colonel Thornton to pump water from the well below it up to Maidenhatch House, which he had just built. Sadly, he lost his money during the Russian Revolution and the property was sold.

In the centre of the village is the church of St James, which was rebuilt in 1868 though the older tower of 1718 was left standing. The church houses the county's largest collection of hatchments. Hatchments are large diamond-shaped boards painted with the coat of arms of a deceased member of the local gentry. They were paraded at the funeral before being hung in the church. Many have long since disappeared, but Pangbourne still proudly displays seven of them, all for members of the Breedon family, the lords of the manor. One on the north wall is unusual in that a skull replaces the usual crest, denoting the last of the Breedon line. The name carried on though for several generations, when a nephew took it up in order to inherit the estate.

To the west of the church is Church Cottage, once the home of the author Kenneth Grahame. Did he see Mole, Ratty, Toad and the rest of the cast of *The Wind in the Willows* as he walked by the river at Pangbourne? In the grounds of Church Cottage is the village lock-up, a small, round building in the perimeter wall of the property. At one time drunks were literally locked-up there until they dried out.

Pingewood

Until 1938, Pingewood was a peaceful little hamlet with country lanes and high hedges, with honeysuckle and dog roses intertwined. This hidden past is still alive in the memory of local residents.

In the centre of the hamlet was Kirton's Farm, 13 cottages, a Church school, large village green with Coronation seat, and Moore's Farm – a smallholding. There was also a large pond, dug out when the railway bridge was built. Around the copse were more cottages, all being pulled down under a system the old folk called 'quit-rent'. In one of these lived a woman reputed to be a witch. A little further out was Cottage Lane, farm buildings, and cottages. This was the short way to walk to Reading, Knights Farm, Pleasant View, Kennet Cottages, The Cunning Man and White Swan public houses, and the blacksmith's, where Mr Nightingale would allow the children to pump the bellows as a treat.

On the bridge over the river Kennet Mr Monty Hawkins would sit for hours making baskets from sticks cut from the withy beds.

Farming was mixed. Heavy horses were bred at Kirtons Farm and took many prizes at shows. The cows and horses would walk the lanes twice a day, coming and going from farms to meadows. When the steam trains passed through, they would sometimes set light to the standing corn, and all the villagers would unite with brooms and sacks to beat out the flames. One postman had a donkey to carry his post bag. In the early days the farmers would take their grain to Burghfield Mill or Calcot Mill. These were run by two brothers named Dewe. Some of the local girls worked in the mill houses.

Through the middle of the village ran a ditch, under an arch called 'Johnny's Arch' – this ditch never ran dry, and the children fished for tiddlers with jam jars on a string. Nearby was a row of eleven elm trees. Watercress was gathered in season. The M4 now runs along this spot!

The keeper and woodsman who worked for Mr Benyon lived in the cottages facing the green. The keeper, Mr Cook, would rear game birds for Mr Benyon, setting the eggs under chickens in his garden, and moving the young birds to a wired enclosure in a nearby meadow, then into the copse where he had a high wheeled wagon to shelter in whilst he fed and looked after them until they were able to fend for themselves.

The copse would be yellow with primroses in spring, with patches of blue or white violets. Although the woods were private, the children would sneak in to pick the flowers until they were chased out by the keeper. Sadly the flowers no longer grow there.

Gypsies were regular visitors to the village. They would camp near Kirtons Farm and come for the pea picking. The horses would be attached to long chains with heavy blocks on the end, to allow them to graze the road side, but be easy to catch. The ladies would sell pegs in the district which they would make sitting around their camp fires in the evenings. At apple harvest time, Mrs Wicks would stand in the road outside her bungalow with her white pinny full of apples, which she would drop for the school children. They would scramble for the apples to enjoy eating on the way home.

Another character was the mole catcher. He wore a moleskin waistcoat. He would call at a cottage with his can and tea, for boiling water. The railwaymen also fetched their pails of drinking water from the village, and the gypsies – who were never any trouble and always ready for a friendly chat. Joan Lambourne, who was born in Kennet Cottages in 1923, remembers vividly the floods that came regularly. The lock keeper sent a message when the river was about to burst its banks. Within half an hour the water would come rushing up the road into the houses. The furniture would have been hurriedly raised on blocks or taken upstairs. Sometimes people would be living upstairs for as long as six weeks. Mr Keene, Knights Farm, would deliver milk from a boat, handing it up to the bedroom windows with a long handled tool. Mr Jim Stroud would do the same, delivering bread. When the water level dropped a little, Mr Percy Hannington would collect children, with a horse and wagon, for school.

The church school was the heart of the village, with regular Sunday service at 3pm – the wooden doors being folded back to show the altar. Communion Sunday mornings as instructed; Sunday school at 2.30pm taken by Mrs Elizabeth Hannington, after the two Miss Springbits left. There was also a prayer meeting at Kirtons Farm – a wagon being pulled into the drive for the preacher to stand on. Miss Goodal was the headmistress. She would run school concerts performed by the children. Afterwards the local talent would have their turn. The school would be packed with people.

Some evenings she would have prayers and hymns – the school would once again be standing room only. She would make hot soup for the children on school days in a large pot, boiling on the coke stove. The children all had their own mugs. Every year Miss Goodal would choose the children with the best voices to train for the singing festival. Pingewood School won the shield seven times, so were very proud when it was awarded to them.

By 1938 the ballast pits had begun, the land being turned into huge lakes. The footpaths vanished, with trees and cowslips, as more land was taken. The school closed in 1958, the farms disappeared – replaced by water-sports. The final blow came when the M4 cut the hamlet in half. Kirtons Farm is now a country club, Knights Farm a restaurant and the old Cunning Man a cafe. The land south of Pingewood is a huge rubbish tip, with lorries continuously thundering by the cottages.

Pinkneys Green

An interesting feature of Pinkneys Green is an estate which started life as a group of pre-fabricated houses built to accommodate an influx of evacuees, mainly from London, during the Second World War. After serving their purpose, they were eventually demolished and, in their place, there was built a council housing estate, the roads of which were named after aircraft bombers such as Blenheim, Halifax, Hampden, Lancaster, Lincoln and Sunderland. It is known affectionately as the Bomber Estate, thus reminding the inhabitants of Pinkneys Green and Maidenhead of the debt owed to the brave men who flew those planes during the unhappy war years.

Another feature of note is All Saints' church, built in 1855 and consecrated in 1857, although, strictly speaking, not actually in Pinkneys Green, but on the fringe.

This church is unique as it is the only one of its kind in the United Kingdom comprising a church, vicarage, stables, schoolmaster's house and school built around a quad-rangle. It was designed by the Victorian architect, G.E. Street, who was responsible for the Law Courts in London.

Much of the terracotta work still to be found decorating buildings in Maidenhead was produced by the Maidenhead Brick and Tile Company, at Pinkneys Green. John Kingdom Cooper was involved in the early expansion of the town in the 19th century, together with William Woodbridge who had brickfields in the Princess Street area. Cooper's Brick and Tile Company was still functioning in Pinkneys Green until a few years ago.

Purley

There was a church at Purley when the Normans ruled England. Although, with the exception of the tower, the church of St Mary the Virgin was entirely rebuilt in 1870, there is still the original Norman chancel arch by the organ and the Norman font, unusually carved with the face of Our Lord.

Purley Magna, on part of which Purley Park now stands, once belonged to Edward the Confessor and was held by the Huscarle family from about 1166-1379 and then for nearly 300 years by the St Johns. The arms of Sir John St John, a staunch Royalist who lost three sons in the Civil

War, are engraved on the church tower with the date 1621, and on the north wall of the tower there is a tablet to his wife Jane. On the same wall is an elaborate mural tablet to Anne, first wife of Edward Hyde, later Lord Clarendon, who died 2nd July 1632 aged 20. She was travelling to Wiltshire with her husband when she became ill at Reading and was taken to relatives at Purley Hall (then known as Hyde Hall). There she died of small-pox in premature confinement and was buried in Purley church. On the mural she is holding a baby in her arms and above her is a shield of arms. Edward Hyde's daughter by his second marriage became the wife of James II and the mother of Queen Mary and Queen Anne.

On the south wall of the chancel is a plate in memory of the Rev John Henry Dudley Matthews, rector of Purley from 1902-1914 who was drowned in December 1914 while crossing the Thames above the weir at Mapledurham Lock late one Saturday evening. He was returning home after preaching in Mapledurham church on the text 'The souls of the righteous are in the hands of God.'

In the churchyard are the tombs of Thomas Canning, 1755-1825, brother of the Prime Minister George Canning, and the distinguished artist Frank Spenlove-Spenlove, who first exhibited at the Royal Academy in 1866 and founded the Spenlove School of Modern Art. Cecil Aldin, the well-known painter of hunting scenes who lived in Purley and died in 1935, is commemorated on a brass plate on the south wall of the church.

Purley Hall, originally 'La Hyde' and then 'Hyde Hall', was built in 1609 by Francis Hyde and later owned by Edward Hyde, Earl of Clarendon and Lord Chancellor.

In 1773 it was bought by the Rev Dr Henry Wilder, rector of Sulham. During Dr Wilder's ownership, Purley Hall was let to Warren Hastings, former Governor-General of India, who lived there from 1788-1794 while his long trial for alleged corruption and ill-dealings was in progress. It is said that he prepared his defence there before being acquitted with honour. He also farmed, bred cattle and horses and had a large menagerie brought from abroad – his celebrated Indian Zoo. There is still an Elephant Yard at the Home Farm and a small painting in the house shows it with some of the creatures about the pool below.

The ghosts of Warren Hastings and that of a grey lady or nun were said to haunt Purley Hall; in fact, when Major and Mrs Bradley first lived there the atmosphere of the place was so oppressive that they arranged for a service of exorcism. Today, Purley Hall is again a peaceful and charming mansion set in beautiful grounds. The garden front is largely original and the house looks down on a quiet pool with a flint grotto at the rear.

In the County Record Office is an interesting memorandum by John Wilder dated 5th June 1803 – 'Being desirous to know, as nearly as possible, the exact spot in the dining room at Purley Hall, in which the three parishes of Purley, Sulham and Whitchurch are supposed to meet, I requested the widow Mary Champ, who professed to be perfectly acquainted with it, to point it out to me – she immediately did so in the presence of my father, mother and my sisters Mary Anne and Lucy – the spot marked by piercing a hole in the floor near the southern-most window, looking towards the canal with a dotted circle round it. Mary Champ represented herself to be 90 years of age on the 4th of the preceeding January – she said that she recollected that the original road leading from Pangbourne to Sulham went straight across the ground which was dug out to make the canal, and that when the canal was made the road was turned, and that the lane, called Nan's Lane, was substituted in its stead as the public road to Sulham – as far as she could recollect Mary Champ thought that this alteration took place when she was about ten years of age.'

In the late 19th century Purley Magna estate was owned by Major Anthony Storer. Major Storer was an antiquary and collector and is said to have dominated the village, spending most of his time watching for people landing on the river bank. Although he was only five feet tall, he once threatened to throw Canon Coleridge – a great man of six feet and weighing 18 stone – into the water for daring to land.

On another occasion he spied a group of ladies picnicking in the park and, without listening to their explanations for being there, gathered their crockery and cutlery into the tablecloth and threw it all into the water. Whereupon one of the ladies said – 'Major Storer, will you please thank your wife for inviting us and for lending us the things you have just thrown into the river.'

Historically little seems to be actually known about Purley Lodge – in fact an article in *The Reading Mercury* dated June 1962 states 'This is probably the first time that anything has been written about Purley Lodge...' and suggests that the lack of written evidence could mean that its existence was kept secret intentionally.

Was the house, to all intents and purposes a perfectly normal 18th century residence, once a minor monastery? There is evidence to show that this could have been so.

About eight years ago the present owner of Purley Lodge, Mr Peter Mosley, was repairing his kitchen floor when he discovered an underground passage running in the direction of the river. Could this be the tunnel once believed to have run beneath the river to Mapledurham on the opposite bank? If so was it a means of escape or communication from Mapledurham House built by the Catholic Blount family in 1588, when religious persecution was rampant? Unfortunately the tunnel has now been blocked up but other discoveries in the Lodge support this theory.

A room known simply as 'the chapel' strengthens the

tunnel's religious significance but perhaps an even more conclusive piece of evidence is a holy water stoup in another part of the house. It is situated in a cupboard and carved out of the solid wall and it is still possible to see the cupboard's original function – a form of porch or vestibule to the chapel with the traditional holy water stoup at its entrance.

Although so much of Purley Lodge's true origin is speculation, it is a fact that during the days of Reading Abbey's importance in the area, the Abbot created a number of minor monasteries called cells. One of these was at Purley and was recorded in a survey called Pope Nicolas' Taxation in 1291, so it does seem possible that the chapel could be connected with the site of this ancient cell where monks from Reading Abbey practised their devotions.

Reading

➤ Once the centre of commercial life in Reading, today the Butter Market is nothing but a large traffic island containing public conveniences. After taking your life in your hands to cross the busy streets here, take a moment to look around and a monument of some importance will catch your eye. The slender, fluted triple lamp support standing in the centre of the old market place was erected in 1804 by Mr E. Simeon who was running for Parliamentary office. The most imaginative architect of the time, Sir John Soane, was employed to design it. Now unnoticed, the sad pillar never found favour, and when new was described as 'a paltry gewgaw thing without use or name' erected by one who wished 'to ingratiate himself with the electors'.

The Forbury Gardens are one of the pleasantest places in the centre of Reading. For centuries the grounds of Reading Abbey, it is now a public park for all to enjoy. The famous Reading Lion dominates the gardens, and not surprisingly, for it must be the biggest sculptured lion in the world, weighing16 tons! It was erected to commemorate the soldiers of the Royal Berkshire Regiment who, in 1880, were massacred at the Battle of Maiwand during the Afghan Wars. Unfortunately the lion's stance is incorrect for if he were real he would fall over!

A smaller memorial of much greater importance stands to the south-east of the great lion. This Celtic cross was put up in memory of King Henry I in 1901. King Henry founded Reading Abbey in 1121 and endowed it with the Blessed Hand of St James the Apostle (still to be seen in Marlow RC church). Few people realise however, that the Abbey's High Altar was his final resting place along with eight other members of the Royal Family. Perhaps he still lies there buried beneath St James' school.

Just outside the Forbury Gardens, spanning Abbey Street, stands the old inner gateway of Reading Abbey, the most obvious remains of one of the richest abbeys in the country. The long gallery over the arch was the scene of confrontation between the abbot and the townsfolk, and quarrels were many. The last abbot came to his end right outside the gate in 1539, when, after a mock trial, he was hanged, drawn and quartered for resisting the dissolution of his monastery. The Abbey gateway survived through its municipal use, and in the 18th century was a school. Today it is part of Reading Museum and Art Gallery.

The sad ruins of Reading Abbey lie hidden to the south-east of the Forbury Gardens. Only the shells of the church's south transept, the chapter house, refectory and dormitory remain. The chant of prayers is no longer heard, nor the first utterances of 'Sumer is icumen in', the earliest four-part harmony from Britain, written so long ago within the Abbey cloister. The imposing shadow of

Reading Gaol, the one time 'home' of Oscar Wilde, makes one think instead of the writer's famous ballad.

The Holy Brook still runs beneath the busy streets of Reading. Now mostly roofed over, it once ran through the town open to the fresh air. A natural channel stretching over five miles from Theale to where it rejoins the Kennet just south of the Abbey ruins, the 'Hallowed Brook' served Reading Abbey as its mill stream. The arch of the old mill still spans the brook behind Reading's Central Library in Kings Road, and this is where the best views of the stream are to be had. The townsfolk sometimes used the Holy Brook for less official purposes. When it was polluted by a nearby dye-works, the Abbot condemned the action as blasphemy.

The pathway through St Laurence's churchyard in Reading is a convenient short cut to the Forbury Gardens, which is kept surprisingly busy. A glance to the side of the path will bring into view an unusual wooden memorial commemorating a man who was killed during a whirl-wind!

It reads:

> In Memory of Henry West
> Who lost his life in a Whirlwind at the
> Great Western Railway Station, Reading
> on the 24th of March 1840 Aged 24 years
> Sudden the change. I in a moment fell
> and had not time to bid my friends farewell
> Yet hushed be all complaint, tis sweet, tis blest
> to change Earth's stormy scenes for Endless Rest
> Dear friends prepare, take warning by my fall,
> so shall you hear with joy your Saviour's call.

The wooden rail has had to be renewed three times, the last time in 1971 by Reading Corporation.

The whirlwind struck Reading with sudden force, concentrated around the railway station. The roar of the wind and crashing of timbers echoed around the Friar Street area, though fortunately for the town, young Henry West was the only fatality. He had been working on the lantern on the top of a wooden waiting room being constructed next to the station house. The lantern weighed four tons but it was flipped over easily by the wind, taking poor Henry with it.

Nearby are the mouldings of a window from Reading Abbey, reminding us that the monks themselves built St Laurence's church to serve the people of the town. This area would have often been trod by numerous pilgrims who visited the Abbey to see the hand of St James, for just to the north can be seen the old dormitory of the Abbey hospitium. Here visitors to the Abbey were given free board and lodging for two days and nights. Originally it could have housed some 400 people.

Riseley & Swallowfield

Immediately to the south of Riseley village hall and opposite the Berkshire/Hampshire boundary sign on the B3349 road, the well-defined course of the Devil's Highway Roman road makes a pleasant walk through to Thatcher's Ford, a favourite summer picnic spot.

Roger de Breteuil, who held the manor of Swallowfield in 1071, was the originator of the Domesday survey. Since that time Swallowfield Park has had a rich history of royal associations and many notable personalities of more recent times have stayed in the present house, which dates from 1689. In 1719 Thomas Pitt bought Swallowfield Park with the proceeds of the sale of a very large diamond he had acquired whilst Governor of Madras. Wilkie Collins,

The Italian Gate, Swallowfield Park

on a visit in 1860, was told the story of Diamond Pitt and used it as the basis of *The Moonstone*. The diamond is now in the Louvre museum, Paris.

Present day visitors are welcomed on Wednesday and Thursday afternoons from 1st May to 30th September so 'hidden' features are then on view and those interested may learn more of Swallowfield Park's fascinating history. The octagonal, brick-built dovecote on the approach to the house has a curious feature in the arcaded cattle shelter, which was added to the earlier building, it is thought, in 1844. The dovecote and surrounding courtyard is private property, not open to the public, but can be seen from the driveway.

Over the archway to the coachyard is an interesting single-hand clock and sundial thought to date from 1790. The clock still keeps good time and chimes on the hour.

The Italian Gate is at the entrance to the walled garden, a dogs' cemetery in which one of Charles Dickens' dogs is buried, and many unusual trees are to be found in the grounds.

The church of All Saints dates from 1256. There is a sundial on the south wall to the east of the porch. Mary Mitford is buried in the churchyard near the little gate into the park behind the church. She lived for some time in a cottage in Swallowfield, and died there in 1855. She began writing to earn money, her family suffering from the debts incurred by her spendthrift father, and wrote many plays and sketches of country life. The latter were eventually brought together as *Our Village*, and she occasionally refers to Swallowfield and its parish church. Fans of her books still come to visit her grave.

The site of Beaumes Castle, in a little copse overlooking the daily turmoil on the busy bypass, was the scene of a romantic episode on Good Friday, 1347, when Sir John de Dalton and his party raided the castle to rescue Margery de

Poynings from a marriage, against her will, commanded by King Edward III. Margery was the young widow of Nicholas de la Beche of Aldworth and a great heiress and ward of the king. She and Sir John fled to Basildon where they were married. So great was the sympathy of the country with the lovers that no-one betrayed them on their journey north to Scotland, beyond the jurisdiction of the king.

Ruscombe

◄ There is evidence that the church at Ruscombe was founded between 1091 and 1185. The right of appointment to the living through the centuries lay with the Dean of Salisbury until 1846, when it was vested in the Bishop of Oxford. Built in flint, the chapel was dedicated to St James. It had no land except some which had been given for use as a cemetery.

Small, single, narrow lancet windows in the east, north and south walls of the chancel are probably the original windows. On the south wall the double lancets on modern central and respond shafts are clearly not contemporary with the single lancets.

There are faded paintings of saints on the splays of the windows in the east wall. These are mainly red on a white background and are thought to date from the 13th century, possibly the handiwork of monks from Reading Abbey.

Paintings of winged angels on the splays of windows on the north and south walls and on the sides of the organ pipe loft are the work of the Rev S.P. Macartney, incumbent from 1907 to 1913. The roof of the chancel is heavy and wagon-shaped and thought to date from the 14th century.

On the outside of the south wall of the chancel is a medieval scratch dial or mass clock. This is a rough round sundial which told the time by the position of the shadow cast by a rod fixed into the central hole, on the seven lines cut in the stone radiating from its base. The outer order of the arch is framed by small reddish bricks of Roman origin.

The brick-built tower has been described as 'the finest of the post-Reformation towers in Berkshire.' The weather vane (a replica of the original blown down in a storm in 1852) bears the royal monogram CR (Carolus Rex) and the date 1639, to which year the tower is attributed.

On the north side of the tower a small stone set in the ground records the tragic death in 1729 of Elizabeth Grove, who fell off a ladder whilst taking her father his lunch as he worked to repair the tower.

For the last eight years of his life, Ruscombe was home to William Penn, founder of Pennsylvania. Born in 1644, Penn had a turbulent life, often imprisoned for his Quaker beliefs. He was the son of Admiral William Penn, a friend of the Duke of York, and in 1681 he was granted territory in North America called 'Pensilvania' after his father. Penn sailed there in 1682, and founded the city of Philadelphia, governing it for two years. Although he did revisit America from 1699 to 1701, he spent most of the rest of his life in England. Ruscombe House, opposite Southbury Farm, where he probably lived from 1710 till his death in 1718, was pulled down in 1830 but the council estate of Pennfields preserves his name.

Sandhurst

On 6th August 1887 the *Reading Observer* reported that 'For some time past the need for a Temperance Hall in Sandhurst has been strongly felt by local individuals. That need has now been happily met by the erection of a hall to commemorate Her Majesty's Jubilee. The building is situated at the junction of Crowthorne Road and New Road [now Longdown Road]. The opening of the hall was performed by the Rev J.W. Spear of the Baptist church, Yorktown.' The Temperance Hall was converted into a private house many years ago, but still stands on the left hand side of Longdown Road as you turn in from the Crowthorne Road. Have the owners ever felt the 'influence of temperance' during their residence?

The 'Round House' situated on the top of Mickle Hill, is now surrounded by houses, but when the house was built for Miss Stone there were only gravel pits in the area. The octagonal house was built as a copy of a house Miss Stone had seen in Sweden. She named the house 'Werels', but later the name was changed to Micklehill, which means Foxhill, mickel being the Swedish for fox. The 'Round House' and 'Threepenny Bit House' are local nicknames.

Rectory Farm, situated on the bend of the road opposite the junction with Yateley Lane, might at a casual glance be mistaken for a pair of Victorian cottages. It is in fact one of the oldest buildings in Sandhurst. The interior discloses fine old wooden beams, as hard as iron and as black as pitch, completely irregular in shape, some as thick as 18 inches at one end and only six inches at the other. The oak beams in the kitchen still have the rings for hanging the bacon to be smoked. Outside near the footpath can be seen the old mounting block, very well worn, and carved in the brickwork is the benchmark for height above sea level in Sandhurst.

Sandhurst Police Station was completed in 1893 in Lower Church Road, in the memory of some older Sandhurst men, and was manned by Police Sergeant Salter, who would put lads in the cells to cool off if he thought their skylarking warranted it. The police station was converted into four flats for residential use in 1985, and the bars have been removed from the windows of the cells!

'Rackstraws', the busy pub and restaurant, attracts all the attention, but hidden away is the old Rackstraws Farm (Antrims Farm), dating back over 200 years. It was the home of John Rackstraw, farmer, who appeared at Reading Assizes in 1798 and obtained an injunction against the lord of the manor to stop him cutting and carrying away sods from the common land, to the detriment of tenants with common pastures. A local hero indeed.

Shinfield

➤ St Mary's church is Norman, though it was restored in the mid 1850s by Sir George Gilbert Scott, when the chancel was extended.

In 1936 the brass commemorating the parents of the authoress Mary Russell Mitford, was discovered under the tiles near the font. Dr George Mitford was an inveterate, and largely unsuccessful, gambler and his family suffered greatly over the years from financial difficulties. His wife Mary was an heiress, whose fortune he soon ran through, and when his daughter won £20,000 on a lottery ticket he did his best to spend that too. He and his wife ended their days in a little cottage nearby at Three Mile Cross, supported only by their daughter's writing talent. When George Mitford died in 1842 he left huge debts, which were paid off by public subscription. Perhaps it is no wonder that Mary herself chose to be buried at Swallowfield, where she lived after his death.

In the village cemetery can be found the grave of Louisa Parsons, who was buried in 1916 with full military honours.

Research has revealed that she trained at the Nightingale School of Nursing, which was founded by Florence Nightingale at St Thomas' Hospital, London, from 1879 to 1883. She subsequently had an astonishing career for a woman of that period, serving with military campaigns round the world and receiving numerous medals and decorations, including the Royal Red Cross from Queen Victoria, the Egypt Medal and Bar presented by the Khedive, the Service Award of the Spanish American War and the Queen's Medal of the South Africa War.

For a time she nursed in America, becoming the Director of the newly established Nurse Training School, which bears her name, at the University of Maryland. Correspondence between the local history society and Maryland revealed their enthusiasm for Miss Parsons and her work, and LHS members were delighted in 1989 to welcome a contingent of nurses and friends from Maryland, who had included a visit to Louisa Parsons' grave at Shinfield in their holiday tour in this country.

The grave lies just to the left of the entrance to the Shinfield Cemetery, which can be found by taking a path opposite the church hall in Church Lane.

Slough

Few think of Slough as an historic town, but there are many ancient sites within its boundaries and the hamlet from which it grew had a history going back over 700 years. When work was going on on the Trading Estate, a number of broken Bronze Age weapons were found, thought to have come from the store of a smith, who would have melted them down to reuse the metal.

In the 18th century Slough was an important staging post on the Bath Road. Daniel Defoe travelled this way and could not understand how all the inns in the hamlet made a living, 'especially as they are opposed by the two famous new ones of the Castle and the Windmill, a little way out of Slough, which are much more delightfully situated, and have better Accommodations'.

The Castle and the Windmill in fact became the most renowned of the local hostelries. They served not only as coaching inns, but as public meeting places, and had pleasure grounds and gardens laid out around them. In 1773 the Colnbrook Turnpike Trustees, who were responsible for the road through Slough, met at the Castle for dinner. It was a meal which has gone down in local history, for five of the eight men present that night died within the next few days. At the time the tragedy was blamed on the possibility of infection caused by a pauper who had been brought before them in their capacity as magistrates beforehand, and it was only many years later, when the landlady Mrs Partridge died, that the truth came out. The turtle soup had been cooked in a copper pan which had become green with verdigris. Left in the pot overnight, the soup had become a lethal brew, supped in innocence by the Colnbrook Trustees.

An 18th century milestone of the Colnbrook Turnpike Trust still stands at Everitt's Corner.

Travellers on the Bath Road must have been intrigued by the sight of an enormous telescope as they reached Slough. A symbolic sculpture erected in front of a block of offices in Slough is now all there is to tell that here stood the home of the famous astronomer Sir William Herschel.

William Herschel had come to England from Hanover in the 1750s as an army musician, but his fascination with astronomy led him in 1781 to discover the planet Uranus. A year later George III appointed him his private astronomer, and it was at Slough that he continued his studies. He worked with his sister Caroline at Observatory House in Windsor Road, which was demolished in the 1960s. Caroline's contribution was significant, though she is seldom remembered, discovering in her own right eight new comets and various other nebulae and star clusters. In 1828 the Royal Astronomical Society awarded her the Gold Medal.

Caroline returned to Hanover in 1822, but William married in Slough and is buried in St Lawrence's church. His son was born here and he too became a renowned astronomer, continuing his father's research. Sir William is remembered by the six-pointed star on the black horse which supports the County Arms of Berkshire.

To the north of St Lawrence's church, a memorial slab records that 'Here Lies the Body of Sarah Bramstone of Eton, spinster, a person who dared to be Just in the Reign of George the second. Obijt. Jany ye 30th 1765. AEtat 77.' Sarah must have been a lady of strong character to deserve such an epitaph. Was George II's reign really quite so bad? The lines may refer to the Duke of Cumberland's unjust reprisals after the Battle of Culloden, so was Sarah perhaps a secret Jacobite?

Slough railway station opened in 1840 and because for some years it was the closest station to Windsor it was used by the rich and famous. The Royal Hotel was built opposite.

Slough railway station was one of the first in the county to have the telegraph installed, though no-one save the railway could see much use for this new-fangled invention. Then in 1845 one John Tawell poisoned his mistress in Slough. The murder was quickly discovered by neighbours who saw John leaving the scene, but he still managed to escape to London by train. However, his description was hurriedly telegraphed ahead to the police and he was soon arrested. Slough station had made history.

A man who must have brought comfort to many athletes, James Elliman, was making his original embrocation for horses in a shed at the back of his linen draper's shop in Buckingham Place in the 1850s. His son went on to open a factory in Chandos Street 20 years later. The family gave generously to the town, including the first fire station and a new steam fire engine, and £10,000 towards enlarging St Mary's church. Salt Hill Playing Fields were created on land provided by the Ellimans, and metal boundary posts with the initials JE were erected around the perimeter.

Once well known for curing eye complaints, Slough's only Holy Well is now neglected and difficult to find. But follow the footpath south-west of the Bath Road near where it joins Montem Lane and after a while you will see a small spring issuing from the opposite bank of the Chalvey brook. This is Queen Anne's Well, so called because it was once patronised by the Royal lady of that name. She had the well encased in a stone-lined trough with a headstone, which sadly is no longer to be seen.

Sonning

➤ Several interesting and unusual wind vanes can be found in the beautiful village of Sonning. The most notable one is that on the Deanery, of a Dean preaching to empty pews.

The Deanery was built for Edward Hudson, the owner of *Country Life*, in 1901, and was designed by Sir Edwin Lutyens. It is behind the original ancient wall and near the site of the residence of the Deans of Salisbury, who maintained a presence here from the 11th to the 16th century. Sonning was also a palace of the Bishops of Salisbury, having belonged to the Church since the 7th century. Lutyens called the vane the 'Unpopular Priest', because he never speaks the truth yet turns with every wind!

The 'Unpopular Priest' had an interesting counterpart in Butts Hill Road on a house used for several years as the vicarage for Woodley church. It was identical except that the pews were occupied. The comparison was naturally a source of speculation.

In Pound Lane the vane of the Ladies Old Golf Course still remains, close to its original site, which was in front of the clubhouse.

Pearson Road contributes a man at work, presumably bricklaying, and close by is another vane about which there is no positive information, though it has a distinctly heraldic flavour.

There was in all probability a Saxon church here but St Andrew's is Norman, built close to the river and so accessible from the road to the bridge. It has some interesting memorials inside. On the chancel floor is a wonderful brass to Sir Laurence Fyton, a bailiff of Sonning, who died in 1434. He is 38 inches tall, dressed in armour, his hands pressed together in prayer, and a kind of sickle-shaped 'speech bubble' curves over his head. There are several other brasses in the same area. Of the other monuments, perhaps the most intriguing is the row of six little 16th century figures, kneeling one behind the other, in the south chancel aisle. The Rich memorial in the tower was, according to Pevsner, described in 1853 as 'the vilest paganism imaginable'!

Speen

◣ St Mary's church dates back to Saxon times, though much of the present building is medieval and 19th century. It has several interesting monuments inside, including one to a Piedmontese gentleman who died here in 1597, John Baptiste Castillion.

When you walk by the church, look to the left: there is a wall with a door. A local lady remembers seeing the door 'open' each Sunday. The villagers would watch the 'parade' from the household to the other side of the wall.

The house-owners advanced, in their Sunday-best clothes, followed by their servants, in crisp uniforms, with white stiff starched aprons, caps and cuffs. They advanced towards the church in order of seniority. In church they were seated, again with seniority in mind: the so-called 'toffs' in the front pews with their servants, and the local villagers seated at the back of the church.

In those days, absence from church service must carry a good excuse. The vicar and Squire Best chased up the absentees! They demanded reasons for such behaviour. This was up to, and after, the First World War.

The 'Little Angel', near the footpath in the churchyard, was the memorial to the little daughter of a local doctor, who was heartbroken when she died. 'In our youth the little angel was snowy-white. We used to pause there, to remember all the little children in our own family who had died: our own 'Two-Minutes Silence'. The little angel seemed almost like a cenotaph – a visual aid to young minds'.

Also buried in the churchyard is James Murray, a coachman on the Bath Road who died at the age of 46 in 1796. He seems not to have enjoyed his work, which must indeed have been hard and dangerous at times, for his epitaph reads:

> 'Tho' while on earth I did remain
> I was reproach and scorn by men
> But now am numbered with the saints
> And saf'd of all my long complaints'.

Speenhamland

Speenhamland today forms the northern part of Newbury, around the Broadway area, but until it was brought within the borough boundaries in 1878 it was a separate village. From the 17th century until the advent of the railways, it was one of the most important coaching centres in the country, being midway between London and Bath on the Great Bath Road. Over 30 coaches a day pulled in here, many breaking their journey overnight.

Coaching and inns were inseparable. Horses had to be changed or rested every ten miles or so, and passengers expected to find refreshment, accommodation, and security from the hazards of the open road. Some of the great Speenhamland inns were the Chequers and the Bacon Arms, both still hotels today, the Bear, the Lamb and Flag and the King's Arms. Probably the most famous, however, was the George and Pelican.

'The famous inn at Speenhamland
That stands below the hill,
May well be called the Pelican
From its enormous bill.'

An 18th century actor, James Quin, famous for his huge appetite for food and wine, is said to have scratched these lines on a window at the inn. Many famous people stayed there including Admiral Lord Nelson, the Pelican being known as one of the best inns on the Bath Road.

Speenhamland, however, has gone into the history books not so much for its coaching pre-eminence, as for a meeting of Berkshire magistrates held at the George and Pelican in 1795.

The late 18th century was a terrible time for the poor of England, many of whom faced death by starvation. The reasons for their plight were numerous – the enclosures, the very bad harvests of the 1790s, the French Wars which hampered the importing of corn, and so on. The price of a loaf of bread soared beyond the means of many rural families.

In May 1795, Berkshire magistrates were called together at Speenhamland to fix a living wage in relation to the price of bread. However, instead of doing this they drew up a scale whereby each member of a family would receive a certain amount out of the parish rates, according to the price of a loaf. Therefore, instead of farmers being forced to pay a living wage to their labourers, the parish was to supplement low wages and make the labourer, in effect, a pauper, dependent on hand-outs. This scale was adopted by magistrates throughout almost all the counties of England, and became known as the 'Speenhamland Act'. Many historians have seen it as one of the main causes of the increasingly bitter lot of the rural labourer which would mark the 19th century.

The George and Pelican is sadly long gone, though the Pelican Yard is still to be found, off London Road.

Streatley

◣ An area at the top of Streatley Hill, adjacent to Westridge, was once named 'Up'. It is shown thus on the Moule map of Berkshire of 1848. In 1960 the signpost opposite Elm Lodge, beside the bus stop, bore a sign 'Up Streatley Hill'. This signpost was subsequently changed by authorities ignorant of, or insensitive to, the historical connection.

The ancient Place Manor was once used to accommodate bishops and others when passing through the district. Its past importance is demonstrated by the adjacent large

116

dovecote, dating from the 14th century. Place Manor is reported to be haunted. It is said that the ghost of a young woman with a baby in her arms has been seen twice in recent times. Another ghost story comes from Warren Farm, where an old shepherd used to see the ghost of his wife tripping around the garden in her nightie. Subsequent research discovered a blonde-haired lady discreetly but unorthodoxly buried close at hand!

The Romans built a causeway across the river Thames between Goring and Streatley, which was usable until Goring Lock was built in 1787. The last surviving rhymer weir on the Lower Thames is here at Streatley. The rhymer was a primitive type of weir, composed of upright posts supported by a   horizontal beam. Small wooden paddles resting against the posts retain the water.

Streatley once boasted a picturesque mill. It was much photographed and painted. In 1922 it became a hydro-electric power station supplying electricity to the district. In 1926 it was unfortunately destroyed by fire.

Towards the end of his life the poet Laurence Binyon lived at Streatley. He is best remembered for the poem '*For the Fallen*', which has become such an inseparable part of Remembrance Sunday –

'They shall grow not old
As we that are left grow old.'

Sulham

➤ Overlooking the M4 motorway like a soldier on watch, stands an ancient pigeon tower. The brick construction is perched on the slope of farmland just above Nunhide Farm, Sulham, and can be reached by a public footpath via Turnhams' Farm or Sulham church. The top

117

section is enclosed and to one side there appears to have been a doorway just above head height, which may have had steps leading to it. This is now bricked up. Under this the tower has two open arches so that you can walk underneath.

There has been much speculation as to its origins. Some say it was a look-out tower or beacon built during the Napoleonic Wars; others refer to it as a 'dovecote'. However, it seems more likely to have been nothing more than a 'folly' built by the Wilder family, who were the main landowners in Sulham for 300 years. The Rev John Wilder was rector at the church of St Nicholas he rebuilt in 1838, for 56 years.

From the tower magnificent views of the Sulham valley can be seen, which is, apart from the motorway to the left, an unspoilt area where two streams, the Pang and Sulham brook, run as neighbours until they reach the Thames. The woods around the tower and to the right are mainly beech and well known locally as particularly good areas for fungi. They provide homes for many badgers.

Fungi in the beech woods at Sulham

Sunningdale

➤ There has been so much building in and around Sunningdale that it no longer resembles the picture most people have in their minds of a typical village, except perhaps for the original area with the school, now a primary school, and parish church at its centre.

About half way between the two in Church Road is a small letter box, situated outside a shop which was for over 40 years the village post office.

The church of Holy Trinity is not old as churches go, but is a fine example of Victorian building and is worth a visit. Wander around the churchyard and you will find a grave which at one time was encircled by a low chain linked to bronze lion heads at each corner, sadly broken off and stolen a few years ago. The inscription tells you that this is the grave of Prince Victor of Hohenlohe and his wife. Prince Victor was a nephew of Queen Victoria and it was whilst attending his funeral that the Duke of Clarence caught the cold which, turning to pneumonia, caused his death. The consequence of this was that his younger brother in due course succeeded to the throne, becoming King George V.

The original church was built in 1839-40 and was enlarged in 1887 as a memorial to the Golden Jubilee of Queen Victoria. Outside on the west wall is the memorial stone laid on 13th June 1887 by HRH the Prince of Wales, placed above that of the original church laid by HRH Princess Augusta in the third year of Queen Victoria's reign. As you enter the church, note the wrought iron hinges on the doors. Just inside is a fine alabaster bas-relief memorial to Prince Victor of Hohenlohe executed by his daughter, Countess Feodora Gleichen.

The vicar from 1857-1884 was the Rev W. C. Raffles Flint and the screen at the entrance to the chancel is a memorial to him. In 1860 he added a chancel and chapel to the original small church, now incorporated in the enlarged building, as a memorial to his near relatives, Sir Stamford and Lady Raffles. Sir Stamford Raffles was one of the founders of the Zoological Gardens, Regent's Park and at one time Governor of the Straits Settlements. Some readers of this may have stayed, in these days of world wide holiday travel, at the Raffles Hotel in Singapore quite oblivious that there was any connection with Sunningdale in the eastern corner of Berkshire.

When you have finished looking round inside, as you emerge from the west door notice an old tombstone just outside. This marks the burial place of Mr Plant, who gave the land for the building of a parish church. Many wedding groups assemble around here for their photographs quite unaware that, but for this man, there might not have been a church in this particular locality.

Theale

Dominating Theale is its 19th century church, Holy Trinity, more impressive without than within. With two towers and the round window of the pinnacled west front, and a third tall tower making an archway through which we can walk, it is as if the architect drew his inspiration from Salisbury Cathedral. The inside is very colourful, with painted patterns covering the walls and the vaulted nave roof, and chancel windows of New Testament scenes and St George with his Dragon. The benches have finely carved poppy heads. But what attracts most is the 15th century stone shrine moved here from Magdalen College, Oxford, by Dr Routh, the College President, to screen the tomb of his sister, Sophia Sheppard, who gave Theale all this new church, except the chancel. She died in 1848, but has a brass portrait on her tomb in the fashion of a medieval brass. A doorway lets us behind the shrine's seven bays and there we see her in a flowing robe with a veil over her head and a dog at her feet.

The 14th century building which is now the Old Lambe Motel was the original Lamb Inn. The present Lamb was built at the beginning of the 19th century, and took its name from the original, which was for many years known as the Old Lamb Teahouse. As a motel the Old Lambe has retained its thatched roof and ship's timbers. A fine open fireplace and the original beer cellars are still there. Scratched on one of the leaded window panes is the date 1704.

The A4 Bath Road, which was a coaching route from London to Bath, runs through the centre of Theale. Stage coaches stopped at the inns, usually the Falcon or the Crown, for 'cakes and ale', but the horses would be watered at one of the pumps positioned at the roadside. One old pump still stands at the western end of the village, and although rusting slightly is still kept painted and is cared for by a local resident.

At one time Theale could boast two Victorian post boxes, one set in a wall at North Street and the other by the gates of the parish church. Unfortunately the post box at North Street has succumbed to the present day disease of vandalism, but the other still remains in good repair in the wall of the church. A few years ago, residents were unable to use this box because a family of field mice had set up home, making a cosy nest of chewed-up letters. Queen Victoria would not have been amused.

There is a very fine oast or malt house situated at the rear of the old Theale Brewery buildings, which are believed to have been built in the 1820s for one Jasper Draper. Although archaeologists believe the malt house to be an

Nineteenth century coaching pump, Theale

older structure than the brewery buildings themselves, because it was unusual for a brewery business to have its own malt house, Draper was probably a maltster long before he started brewing.

In 1854 the brewery was taken over by the Blatch family and remained in their possession until 1965 when Ind Coope bought the buildings and the malt house.

The malt house cannot be seen from the High Street, but a public footpath at the eastern end of the street runs towards the rear of the old brewery and some of the other lovely old red brick buildings can also be viewed.

Tilehurst

Tilehurst has always been closely connected with Reading; indeed, it was described as a 'hamlet of Reading' as far back as 1291. Even so, it was only brought into the borough boundaries in 1911, and before that was a rural village with a long history of tile making.

The old village was centred around the 13th century church of St Michael, with the lord of the manor living at Calcot Park. St Michael's has an ornate memorial to a merchant, originally from Utrecht, called Sir Peter Vanlore, who died in 1627. He and his wife lie side by side, their hands held up in prayer, while at the side of them are their children, some carrying skulls to denote that they too sleep here.

At the end of the 19th century two successful firms set up business here. Tilehurst Potteries was founded in 1885 by Samuel Wheeler at Kentwood Hill, producing flower pots and roofing tiles, and S. & E. Collier came to Grovelands. Collier's, whose bricks can still be seen today all over Reading, was still in business up to the 1960s and was a major manufacturer of bricks, tiles and terracotta. There are no kilns today in Tilehurst, but a link with the past has been retained in the name of a housing estate, The Potteries.

The wrought-iron gates, made in the early 1970s by a retired blacksmith, are the entrance to an early Victorian house in old Tilehurst village.

The gates are made in three dimensions, with roses and bells on one, and chrysanthemums and bells on the other. They are quite outstanding to look at in this age of harsh shapes and angles. Also, at the back of the house is a wishing well and a wall lamp, made in the old street-lamp style; both of these are made in wrought iron.

Twyford

The first definite recorded reference to a water mill in Twyford is in 1363, but there is an earlier reference to 'Wimund the miller of Tuiford' in 1163, thought to be of the same site. Not until 1624 however, when William Hide the miller died, is there any concrete reference to a flour mill on the banks of the Loddon in Twyford.

In 1799 Thomas Billinge, a miller from Macclesfield, bought Twyford grist mill along with several other properties in the village. Some seven years later three buildings were erected by the mill and silk milling began. Thomas and his wife Elizabeth spent much time renovating and eventually living in the Mill House opposite the mill. Alongside they built five three-storey weavers' cottages with especially large windows on the top floor where the weavers worked. Mill House can still be seen today but the weavers' cottages were demolished in 1937.

One interesting snippet about the silk mill is that in September 1827 there was a robbery. 'A gang of thieves' stole bales of raw silk valued between £600 and £700; but the horse, frightened by something, gibbed and backed the loaded cart into the river Loddon. The commotion woke nearby residents and the thieves made off, it is thought by stage, to Newbury. Rewards of £10 from the Hurst Association and £20 from Mr Billinge were offered for information. Later it was learned that five cwt of cheese had been stolen, prior to the robbery, from a waggon at Hare Hatch – thought to have been the work of the same gang. A month later the *Reading Mercury* published a paragraph that two suspects were being questioned by the London police, but the final outcome was never published.

Although in the 1820s Reading and Henley silk mills closed due to the imports of cheap raw silk, the Billinge family kept Twyford's mill working until 1845. It was then sold to William Davis, corn miller.

The corn mill has been much beset by disastrous fires, mainly due to the combustible nature of its produce. In 1875, after a fire in the village, Lawrence Davis founded the Twyford Fire Brigade, but even this did not save his mill some 16 years later when the entire structure was destroyed - water was in short supply because the ponds were frozen. A new and larger brick mill was built to the exacting fire regulations of the day, water still being the main power supply, supplemented by steam, later replaced by gas and then diesel. The mill had its own railway siding, corn coming by rail and the processed material distributed the same way. The Berks, Bucks and Oxon Farmers, who bought the mill in 1927, completely modernised it in 1958, using it for compounding livestock feed. Fire struck again most spectacularly in 1976, the flames topping the 80ft silos. It completely destroyed the old building, but fortunately the cottages opposite escaped with only singed paint.

Today a huge corrugated building is the modern mill, not exactly a thing of beauty but a very busy working mill yet again built to today's fire standards.

Dr William Gordon Stables (1837-1910) was a writer, adventurer and a truly notable man. After medical training at Aberdeen University he sailed far and wide as a ship's doctor. This journeying ruined his health and in 1870 he came to Twyford to spend his life as an author, adviser on medical matters and naturalist. His travels on the high seas gave him ready-made subjects for his stories. He was an early contributor to *Boys' Own Paper* with both adventure stories and advice on health. He had published over 100 books for boys.

He had a great love of nature of all sorts; his home at Twyford was aptly called 'The Jungle'. In the garden was a little wooden summer-house – 'The Wigwam' – where he wrote both in summer and in winter when only an old tartan shawl gave him extra warmth. At one time he had a small veterinary practice at 'The Jungle'.

He still had one ambition. In 1885 he had built, by the Bristol Waggon Co, a 20ft by 7ft caravan. This very elaborate (for the time) vehicle can still be seen today in the Industrial Museum, Bristol. In it he packed, as well as the essential things, a tiny harmonium, a piano stool, a fiddle and a guitar. Foley, his valet and general factotum, slept in the tiny aft cabin on two door mats and a thin cork mattress while his Newfoundland dog, Hurricane Bob, slept in the front of the waggon. John, the groom, sometimes slept at the inn where the horses, Cornflower and Polly Peasblossom, were stabled, but more often he slept in a tent with the horses tethered close by. A white cockatoo completed the menage.

When they set off on their travels, bowler-hatted Foley rode in front on a tricycle to give warning of the coming van, while John in top hat and gloves had charge of the horses. Dr Stables cut quite an extraordinary sight in tam o'shanter and kilt plus his old shawl in inclement weather.

They travelled for six months at a time following Stables' fancy. The very first journey, a 1,300 mile expedition, was the basis of his book *The Cruise of the Land Yacht Wanderer*. From this trip the 'Wanderer' returned from Glasgow, sans wheels and springs, by railway wagon. The shattered contents resulted in this being the first and last trip by rail.

In June 1907 the Caravan Club was formed by eleven enthusiastic caravaners and, although not present, Stables was elected their first Vice-President. The 'Wanderer' and its little band was now a well known sight throughout the countryside and his book *Leaves from the Log of a Gentleman Gipsy in a Wayside Camp and Caravan* well sums up the latter years of his life.

For many years the sign of the Wee Waif inn has been associated with the name of Edward Polehampton. On a certain Christmas Eve around 1666 a destitute boy of this name was befriended by the landlord of the Rose and Crown inn at Twyford. The lad was accepted by the family and enjoyed good food, clothing and shelter.

Eventually, so the story goes, the lad made his way to London and, in time, rose from being a penniless wanderer to a man of distinction and wealth. Remembering the kindness he had received when in dire distress, in his will he bequeathed a charity to benefit poor boys of Twyford. The Trust is still in existence and, as well as the Wee Waif, two local schools in Twyford commemorate his name.

It is a charming story, but largely discredited by the Twyford and Ruscombe Local History Society, and others. The prosaic version is that Edward Polehampton was born to well-to-do parents at Hurst (of which Twyford was then a part) in 1652. So, apparently well-connected, it is difficult to understand Polehampton's need for help at the Rose and Crown.

It is a fact that Edward Polehampton, who never married, went to London and, among other achievements, became a well-known painter of portraits and coaches, a teacher of painting, printseller and Captain of Trained Bands. In his will, dated 27th July 1721, he provided an annuity 'for ever' for the boys of Twyford. A study of a copy of the will does not give credence to the 'waif' version of the story.

It is a pity there is scepticism about such a moving tale. Nevertheless, legends, myths and stories handed down orally usually have some factual basis. Perhaps there was after all a 'wee waif' who found help and comfort in Twyford and who was the inspiration for the Wee Waif inn sign.

Warfield

The village of Warfield has a rather unusual war memorial, for, in 1919-20, by public subscription, five acres of meadowland were purchased in the centre of the village, and designated as the memorial to the men of Warfield who had died in the First World War.

This has always been known as the Memorial Ground, and has been a source of pleasure for all the village. All outdoor village events are held there, including the annual village fete and the pumpkin show. It is the home of the cricket club and a football club. There is a well-equipped pavilion, and a children's play area. The Ground is administered by trustees.

There used to be an oaken arch, with appropriate wording traversing the crosspiece, at the entrance at the corner of Osborne Lane, but this was accidentally knocked down by a high vehicle after a village fete many years ago. In 1975, the Fete committee of the day decided to erect a more permanent entrance, and earmarked the profit of two years' fetes to this end. It was designed by the then chairman, Tony Ingram, who persuaded James Moss and Sons to build it. It now takes the form of a lych gate, flanked by low walls, in which are incorporated incised stone tablets, one commemorating the fallen of the two world wars: 'In memory of the men of Warfield who gave their lives in two world wars, 1914-18; 1939-45'; and the other the Silver Jubilee 'Commemorating the Silver Jubilee of HM, Queen Elizabeth II, June 1977'. A very small plaque also indicates 'This Community is recorded in the Domesday Book 1086', and was placed there to celebrate 900 years of Norman heritage.

This memorial gateway is restricted to pedestrians only, a new vehicle entrance having been opened at the far end of the field. The grass bank between the gateway and the road has, for several years, been planted with flowers by the Warfield Brownies, who still tend them.

The Cricketers is a very old village inn. Years ago it was known locally as The Orchard House, being surrounded by fruit trees.

The gamekeepers from nearby Warfield Park used the inn and the story goes that the poachers would peer through the windows, see the gamekeepers having a good time and would go off to the park – poaching! Access to the inn in those days was a footpath, known as Cricketers Lane.

The cellars are the best in Berkshire and beer was stood for a year. At the end of one cellar is a well. This keeps the cellar very cool. There are many wells in the Cricketers' grounds. No deeds have ever been found, so the actual age of the inn is not known.

Robert Henry Claude Harris was a local postman in Warfield, living with his parents, but sadly, in 1932, at the age of 24, he died of a blood disorder. He was buried in the village churchyard, and his grieving parents erected a monument to him, in the form of a postbox. Objections were raised to this, and it finally had to be removed from the churchyard.

In 1933, Mr and Mrs Harris moved to a newly-built bungalow in the village, and had a marble memorial stone placed in the brickwork in the front of the building, with the initials 'RCH'. It remains there to this day – a permanent memorial to a beloved son.

The name of the property? 'Rosemary' – for remembrance.

Wargrave

The first mention of the manor or village of Wargrave comes in the Domesday Book 1086. Wargrave, valued at £27 6s 8d, was one of the richest and most populous villages in East Berkshire at that time. There was a mill on the Loddon river and three fisheries, which would have been weirs or eel traps. Wargrave stood on the edge of Windsor Forest surrounded by groves or thickets of trees and bushes. Thus the early name Weirgrove was formed. The name for the green in the centre of the village, Mill Green, was derived from the mill on the river. It seems appropriate to write of Mill Green in this book as it is not immediately visible to the casual visitor to Wargrave. A little walk from the main Henley Road via Station Road or Church Street will discover this little piece of 'Hidden Berkshire'.

Situated at the side of Mill Green stands Wargrave Court. Almost certainly the manor house, its origins date back to the 15th century, although the exposed timberwork on the gables is part of alterations carried out in Victorian or Edwardian times. There is a clue to the real age of the house in the old tile roof with the change in ridge height, but the most compelling evidence lies within the

The Druids' Temple at Wargrave

house. The size and quality of the frame indicates that the house was built by someone of some substance; this together with its location near the church supports the proposition that it was the manor house.

In St Mary's churchyard at the west side of Mill Green stands the Hannen Columbarium. It has an interesting interior with a domed ceiling, lined with ceramic slip tiles over brick barrel vaults, and this on a semicircular colonnade of six columns with a moulded frieze, designed by Sir Edwin Lutyens in 1906. Lutyens also designed the Portland stone war memorial situated at the entrance to Mill Green, and in conjunction with the Hannen family firm, the Cenotaph in Whitehall.

The Mill Green has a strong association with an 18th century character called Jack Fletcher, who was known as the Wargrave Fool. He had amazing powers of mimicry. A Mrs George Berkeley described him thus:

'It was his practice to attend various churches in the neighbourhood, and then after hearing the sermon he was not only able to repeat it verbatim, but to imitate the voice of the preacher so closely that a person in the next room would be led to infer it was the preacher himself.'

Perhaps he repeated the sermons heard in St Mary's church on Mill Green!

The Bull Inn, to be found on the corner of the main Henley Road and Church Street, two minutes walk from the green, was undoubtedly one of Jack Fletcher's watering places. Some odd happenings have been reported at the Bull, especially around Henley Regatta time. One visitor refused to sleep in his room after hearing the continual lament of a woman calling for her child. A woman was known to have died in childbirth at the Bull. Many strange happenings have occurred: doors opening and closing and the air becoming unnaturally cold at the same time; children's cries have been heard and the vision of a woman has been seen to pass through the door of the long bedroom; while the figure of a man wearing a long black cloak and hat has been seen to drift through the bar. Why not pop in and ask the landlord why his beer pumps stop and start for no reason at all?

Travelling along the A321 from Wargrave to Henley, the narrow road funnels even narrower over a humped-back bridge lined with stones said to be from Reading Abbey. It crosses Happy Valley, a fold in the hills by the Thames on the estate once owned by General Henry Conway, Governor of Jersey. In 1788, 45 even larger stones were unloaded here – a complete 'Druids Temple' – given to General Conway by the people of Jersey in recognition of his services to the island. The huge granite blocks had been shipped from St Helier to London at the General's own expense and then transferred to Thames barges for an extremely hazardous week-long journey up the Thames to Park Place. It is possible that some of the stones may have been lost en route, for it is known that some are missing.

The stones were erected in a 25 ft circle in the garden close to his huge mansion (said to have 44 bedrooms). Conway lived here with his wife and daughter, Anne, from 1752 until his death in 1795. His daughter, as Anne Damer (her married name) was a well known sculptress and her work can still be seen today in the carved heads of Isis and Thamesis on each side of the central span of Henley Bridge.

Fire destroyed Park Place in 1870 and over the years the estate has been broken-up. Today the Temple stands in the garden of Temple Combe, close by a house designed in 1958 by the American architect Frank Lloyd Wright. It is the only house of his in the country; a very elaborate 'U'-shaped building with rich mahogany timbering, suede panelled walls and marble floors. The estate, now 120 acres, about a fifth of the size of Park Place, came on the market in 1988 valued at £1.65m complete with the dolmen in the garden.

Windsor

If Westminster Abbey were the Pyramids of England, then St George's Chapel, Windsor must surely be the Valley of the Kings. For it is within St George's and not at nearby Frogmore that most of the Sovereigns of this land have chosen to be buried. Here are the tombs of no less than ten Kings, and six of their Queens, along with numerous other Princes and Princesses. From Charles I, the man who tried so hard to retain his throne, to George VI who had it thrust upon him; from the pious Henry VI to the flamboyant Henry VIII, all rest here together for evermore.

Just as colourful, though not so famous, was Sir John Dineley, who is also buried in St George's Chapel. His name was originally Dineley-Goodere, but when he inherited the baronetcy in 1761 he dropped the Goodere name. Not surprisingly, because his father had had his own brother murdered for his money and title, and his elder brother had died insane!

Sir John soon spent what was left of the Dineley fortune, and friends managed to obtain for him a pension and a home as a Poor Knight of Windsor. This order is now known as the Military Knights of Windsor, selected for their distinguished military service. He became well known in Windsor for his eccentric style of dress, but it was his efforts to find a wife which really attracted attention. He believed that, if he could only marry a woman with money, he could set about proving family links with the wealthiest of ancient families. He would, therefore, keep an eye open for a likely looking woman, and hand her a leaflet from a bundle which he always carried with him, setting out his prospects and his marriage proposal. He even went to London in the season to try his luck there. Needless to say, he was not successful and Sir John died a bachelor in 1809 at the age of 80.

Edward III had the famous Round Tower at Windsor Castle built as a meeting place for his newly created Most Noble Order of the Garter. The order had been established at the height of the King's military career with a view to reviving the chivalry of the Round Table and King Arthur's reign. The knoll on which the Round Tower stands was said to have been the original site of the Round Table and meeting place of Lancelot, Gawain and the other goodly knights of old.

In the shadow of the castle walls is the elegant parish church of St John the Baptist. The original church on this site was built in Norman times, and in 1168 documentary reference is made to it maintaining a leper hospital. The old church, however, became unsafe and the present 'Gothick' building replaced it in 1820-22, designed by

Charles Hollis. Inside it has galleries on three sides, so providing seating for about 1,700 people – very necessary in a town which had grown by then to a population of about 10,000, including the garrison. The polygonal apse was added in 1869-73.

Several monuments were saved from the old church, dating back to the 16th century, and there are two interesting treasures. The carved wooden rails in the south chapel were carved by Grinling Gibbons himself, in about 1680, and were in the castle chapel, probably as part of the communion rail, until 1788. The church also has an impressive painting of The Last Supper by the German artist Francis de Cleyn, 1588 - 1658, which also hung at one time in the royal chapel and was a gift to St John's from George III.

One of the first curates of the new church after 1822 was George Augustus Selwyn. He began a school for 19 poor boys in a washerwoman's cottage at the corner of Goswell and Clewer Lane, and though the school itself eventually closed, St Mark's foundation of 1846 carried on its main ideas. Selwyn himself was a brilliant churchman, and went on to become the first, and only, Bishop of New Zealand and Melanesia, founding the church in New Zealand. In 1867 he became Bishop of Lichfield. He was educated at St John's College, Cambridge, and after his death the University founded Selwyn College in his memory. Just as a byline on this distinguished career – he also rowed in the first university boat race in 1829!

Trampled under the feet of hundreds of tourists and townsfolk alike every day, is a clock set into the pavement of Thames Street in Windsor. It lies there as a novel advertisement for a certain nearby jewellers, now closed down, and certainly makes a change from looking up at a church tower to tell the time.

In the forecourt of King Edward VII Hospital stands a statue of the king, erected in 1912. The money for it was raised by a memorial fund, set up following his death. The statue was designed by Countess Feodora Gleichen, granddaughter of Queen Victoria's half-sister, Feodora, Princess Hohenlohe Langenberg. The figure of the king is surrounded, at its base, by four female figures: Cheerfulness, Kindness, Sagacity and Sympathy.

Beware mysterious sounds heard on the night air in Windsor, for they may signal the arrival of Hearne the Hunter and his ghostly Hunt. Hearne was the favourite huntsman of Richard II. When mauled by a deer, he gave his hunting skills to a wizard in return for saving his life. The wizard secured a set of antlers to Hearne's head and it wasn't long before he was back at the peak of health. However, grief-stricken by the loss of his livelihood, he went out into the forest and hanged himself. A tree known as 'Hearne's Oak' still stands on the original site of his natural gibbet. The man himself, complete with antlers, appears beneath the tree whenever the country is in peril. But as it stands almost at the centre of the Home Park, it is impossible to get to, so no-one would ever know of the impending danger!

Winkfield

The village of Winkfield is set in what is believed to be the second largest parish in England, taking in a wide area of what was Windsor Forest, though it is now in danger of becoming joined by housing development to Bracknell New Town.

The church of St Mary was built in about 1300, though its brick tower is of 1629. The ornately carved font is Victorian, from 1863. There are some interesting memorials, including a brass near the pulpit showing Thomas Montague, who died in 1630, distributing alms. A tablet commemorates Thomas Wise, master mason to Charles II, in 1685.

But the most interesting thing about St Mary's is that it has pillars down the middle. These pillars have a tale. They were built in Queen Elizabeth I's reign, but when the church was partly built, the Devil came and pulled it down. Eventually, a pact was made with the Devil, that he could build half the church. So, the pillars were installed again, to divide the church between the Devil's side and the Lord's side. Many old Winkfield people would not be buried on the Devil's side of the church. Even now, when the bride and groom come down the aisle, they have to part company for the pillars.

Wokingham

➤ During the 19th century, the small market town of Wokingham was the Berkshire stronghold for a sport which was very popular at the time – bull baiting.

In 1661, a Mr George Staverton, having been gored by a bull and and hoping no doubt for revenge, charged his estate with £6 a year to provide the people of Wokingham with a bull to be baited. The bull was then to be killed and the meat given to the poor, the hide to be made into shoes for the children.

Many of the townsfolk of Wokingham owned bull dogs and these animals were the objects of much loving care. A victorious dog, that is one which had 'pinned' a bull's nose, was rewarded with a silver collar.

The Staverton bull was always baited on St Thomas' Day, 21st December, although there were several lesser baits during the year.

On 21st December, almost the whole population of the town assembled in the market place – the scene was one of bustle and excitement – every window was filled with expectant faces, men clambered on to the roofs and small boys into the only tree in the market place. Only the most courageous of the spectators ventured into the actual arena with the dog owners. Carriages filled with occupants drew up before the three inns in the market place, the Bush, the Old Rose and the Red Lion. A buzz in the crowd heralded the arrival of Wokingham Corporation, the Alderman, burgesses, town clerk, two sergeants of the Mace, the Mace bearer and two ale tasters. They all assembled in the window of the Red Lion. The baiting could then begin.

The Alderman gave the signal and the bull was brought in. This took twelve strong men pulling on a rope tied around its horns. It was tethered to the ring with a 15 foot chain. The first dog was then let loose and dog and bull studied each other for a few moments; the dog was well aware what was expected of it, he must attack the bull's nose whilst at the same time avoid its horns. On the other hand, the bull's instinct told it to get its horns under the dog to protect its nose. If the dog failed to 'pin' the bull, it would either get its stomach ripped open or be tossed high into the air, maybe to be impaled on railings. When this happened, the crowd screamed, the pickpockets took their opportunity in the chaos to go about their nefarious work, and the unfortunate dog shrieked in agony. Another dog would then be let in to confront the bull, and this went on until the bull was 'pinned', that is until a dog managed to sink its teeth into the bull's nose. At this point the twelve strong men entered the arena again to separate dog from bull.

On one occasion the bull gave a mighty heave and succeeded in pulling up the ring. The twelve men managed at last to recapture it and tethered it to the tree, whereupon it shook the tree so hard that several small boys fell out of it.

Mayhem usually followed the bull baiting with fighting in the streets. This often resulted in spectators being injured as one entry in the parish register notes. 'Martha May, aged 55, injured by fighters after bull baiting, was buried December 31st 1808.'

Bull baiting continued regularly until 1821 when public opinion turned against such a barbaric sport and it was discontinued until 1835. In that year the mob broke into the pen where the Staverton bull was kept and baited it in spite of the efforts of magistrates to stop them. In 1835, an Act was passed prohibiting bull baiting anywhere in the country.

Of the three inns around the market place, only the Red Lion survives in its original position. The Bush has gone, the original Old Rose was burnt down and the present one was built on the opposite side of the market place.

In the graveyard of All Saints' church stands an enormous block of Portland stone known as the Beaver Monument. This monument was erected in 1787 by Mr Benjamin Beaver as a tribute to his wife Elizabeth, whom he loved dearly.

Benjamin and his wife had been greatly saddened by the death of their young nephew, Thomas Leach and the monument bears this warning:

> 'Stop youth, take warning for here lieth also the remains of our beloved nephew, Thomas Leach who was lost July 14th 1761 in swimming in the river Thames near Caversham lock, to the great sorrow of all who knew him. In the 16th year of his age.'

These tributes filled only one side of the huge monument, the other sides are filled with a rambling story relating the fortunes of Benjamin's relatives during the Civil War. They were staunch supporters of the Royalist cause, raising troops of horse and joining with troops raised by other landed gentry of the neighbourhood. But great misfortune befell them, the cause was hopeless. The king was defeated and his loyal followers suffered persecution and the sequestration of their goods. Thomas Bowlen, a coal merchant, had supplied tons of coal to the court at Windsor, was never paid 'and lost his debt of thousands'.

Benjamin concludes by telling the sad story of Henry Dean. He also lost all his money, so that 'he had nothing left but a tenement of £3 a year and he was obliged to earn his living from the age of 50 years (not being used to work) for above 30 years more till his end, by gardening'. It did not seem to do him much harm however for Benjamin adds, 'he was patient, healthy and of a cheerful and honest heart – he died at the age of 85.'

The Molly Millar public house stands not far from Wokingham station. Its inn sign is a picture of a beautiful barmaid, but when the brewers gave the inn the name Molly Millar, was this a case of mistaken identity?

Wokingham had two Mollys, Molly Millar and Molly Mogg. But it was Molly Mogg who was the beautiful barmaid, not Molly Millar. Nowhere is Molly Millar mentioned in the local history books in Wokingham library. On the other hand, there was no difficulty in finding information on Molly Mogg. She was the daughter of John Mogg, the landlord of the Olde Rose Inn and by all accounts strikingly beautiful. So lovely was she that she was immortalised in a ballad – *The Ballad of Molly Mogg or The Fair Maid of the Inn* – written by John Gay and his friends, Alexander Pope, Dean Swift and Sir

John Arbuthnot, when they were detained at the Olde Rose by a violent thunderstorm. The ballad was published in Mist's Journal in 1726. It has even been suggested that Molly Mogg was the model for Polly Peachum, the heroine of John Gay's *The Beggar's Opera*.

But could Molly Millar and Molly Mogg be the same person? Did Molly Mogg marry and become Mrs Molly Millar? The parish register disputes this, it states that Mary (Molly) Mogg died a spinster on Sunday 9th March 1766 at the age of 67.

So who was Molly Millar? The old drovers' road, now a street of houses and factories, is called Molly Millar's Lane. The record office at Shinfield could shed no light on the identity of the mysterious Molly Millar. They said 'Molly Millar's Lane is mentioned in the 1817 enclosure map as a public horse and drift road, 20 ft wide.'

The Molly Millar public house was previously the Station Inn. The name was changed in 1960. So did they get the name wrong?

The local theory is that Molly Millar was simply an old woman who lived in a cottage along the old drovers' road and could be frequently seen gathering sticks for her fire. The drovers got to know her and referred to the road as Molly Millar's lane to distinguish that route from any other which they might take. The name was later adopted by Wokingham council. Wokingham people are inclined to the opinion that to name the public house the Molly Millar was a case of mistaken identity.

Poor Molly Mogg, she had her hour of glory but is now almost forgotton whilst the name of Molly Millar lives on.

Deep in the green fields, on the south side of Wokingham, between the Easthampstead and Finchampstead roads, not a mile away from the incessant traffic passing through the town, is a beautiful and dignified old house, built in 1666 in the reign of Charles II. Over the centuries this building has provided shelter and comfort for 16 poor, honest old men.

It was founded by Henry Lucas, a mathematician and Member of Parliament for Cambridge University, who left £7,000 for the erection and endownment of a hospital in Berkshire. The foundation was to consist of: 'A Chaplain or Master and as many poor men as could be provided for, chosen from the poorest inhabitants of the Forest Division of Berkshire and the Bailiwick of Surrey in or near the forest'.The Master appointed should be: 'A single person, a graduate of the University of Cambridge, and a Master of Arts – a minister lawfully ordained and an orthodox preacher of good life and conversation.'

The Trust was taken over by the Drapers' Company in 1675. In 1676 an order by the Company agreed that a married man could be appointed Master, not necessarily of Cambridge University. John Herdman was the first Master.

The brethren were required to attend Divine Service every morning and evening and on Sabbath days, in the chapel which occupies the east wing of the building; the west wing being the Master's house. A yearly sum of £10 was paid to the brethren and gradually increased over the years.

There is a pleasant walled garden where small plots could be worked by the brethren. In good weather they could walk the field paths into town.

Today, when everyone is entitled to an old age pension the hospital plays a different role. It is now run more as a retirement home, with a number of self-contained flats, with a caring qualified nurse as Matron who is always on call. She visits all of them every day. They are charged a reasonable rent for their very pleasant accommodation. Married couples and women now occupy some flats.

Wokingham Without

◣ St Sebastian's is not a village – it is an ecclesiastical parish in the civil parish of Wokingham Without. The name Wokingham Without is something of a mystery to many people. It was created in 1894 when the parish of Wokingham was split into Wokingham Within and Wokingham Without. The 'Within' has been dropped but the 'Without' has stayed and is used in the old meaning of outside. It is simply that part of Wokingham parish outside the town boundary.

In the days when the heathlands south of Wokingham were only criss-crossed by tracks and rides, there were people who made brooms and besoms from the natural materials of the heath. It is thought about 15 households were so occupied, about 25 males.

Their dwellings were fashioned mainly from peat and birchwood. A few simple tools, supple fingers and a great deal of patience was all that was required for the craft. They valued their independence; a small community of their own.

A day's work ran to approximately ten dozen brooms, stacked head to tail in bundles of twelve, despatched weekly to Reading, and some exported through Bristol.

By the mid 19th century these families were requesting baptism for their children and a local curate began visiting the community. A day school was opened by a Captain Sawyer, who also began collecting money for a church. Eventually St Sebastian's was consecrated by the Bishop of Oxford, on 10th December 1864.

Almost hidden in the hedge beside the Wokingham to Crowthorne road is a stone which tells a sad story. It was erected in 1978 by the Wokingham Without Parish Council. A plaque attached to the stone states, 'This stone marks the spot where Private R. Lockhart died on the 26th July 1855 while on the march from Farnham to Wokingham. Erected by Wokingham Without Parish Council during the Silver Jubilee year of Queen Elizabeth II'. A nearby residential road has been named Soldiers Rise to commemorate the incident.

The old Roman road from London to Silchester passes through the parish. One stretch, known as the Devil's Highway runs alongside the East Berks golf course. In 1920, P. H. Ditchfield the historian wrote 'A little further and we come to the golf links. There I have often seen the Roman milestone which I hope the golfers have left undisturbed.' In the 1930s Canon Coleridge also wrote of a Roman milestone in the wood east of the golf links.

Around 1975, Martin Prescott, a local historian wrote that he could find no evidence at all for such a stone unless it had been confused with the sarsen stone dug up near the site of the Roman road during the building of a large housing estate. This stone, erected beside one of the roads on the new estate, bears the legend 'This ancient stone formerly stood close to this spot marking the boundary of Wokingham with Sandhurst/Crowthorne. [Sandhurst and Crowthorne were at one time just one parish.] The Roman road from Silchester to London ran a few yards to the north of it. Removed and re-erected 6th April 1963'. The stone was named the 'Wulwyn stone'. According to the estate developers, Wulwyn was the name of an officer in the Roman legion which was stationed in this area. So, was the Wulwyn

Wayside stone marking the building of the forest road,
Wokingham Without

stone an old Roman milestone? No-one seems to know for sure. Sadly the stone no longer stands upright, it lies on the ground.

At one time the Great Forest of Windsor covered all this area. In the year 1770 a group of local landowners decided to build a road through the forest linking Windsor with Reading. The road was to be known as The Forest Road and the landowners raised the money to build it. Alas, the Forest Road has now become a casualty of the A329M motorway which has cut through it, leaving one small section as a cul-de-sac. Neglected and weatherbeaten, a large oval stone stands beside this section of the forest road. It lists the names of the landowners who contributed to its building. These are,

The Countess of Leicester.
Lady Hervey.
Mrs Montague.
Mrs Hewer.
Mrs Barram.
Richard Neville Neville.
James Edward Colleton.
Samuel Bowes.
Romsey Bowes and
Richard Palmer.
Surveyed by Mr Basnett 1770.

The monument was originally erected on the estate of the Countess of Leicester but when the Leicester estate was sold, it was moved to its present position. The inscription is now completely obliterated.

The name of the public house the Who'd a Thot It, is said to have been the exclamation of the 1st Duke of Wellington on coming, tired and thirsty, upon an ale house in a clearing in the forest. Originally the inn sign depicted the Duke and his men coming upon the ale house. The present sign however shows men walking on the moon and coming upon a huge bottle of Morland's beer. Who'd a thot it indeed!

Many local people believe that Ambarrow is an ancient burial mound where casualties from a battle against the Danes were buried in a communal grave, but there is no real evidence to support this. It is more likely to be a natural feature. Barrow simply means hill and the alternative Hambro Hill is probably a truer description.

The Wokingham Without Community Association occupies the site of the old Pinewood Hospital. The hospital was built at the beginning of the 20th century for tuberculosis patients sent from London. It was believed at the time that the hospital, set amongst the pinewoods, was extremely beneficial to tuberculosis sufferers. It was then known as the London Open Air Sanatorium. In the First World War it was used for the treatment of Canadian and other casualties from poison gas. In the Second World War it became the 1st New Zealand General Hospital. After the New Zealanders left it was used by Polish forces.

After the war it was turned into a small general hospital to serve the district and continued thus for about 20 years, then it was closed much to the disappointment of the local people. The Ministry of Health tried for years to dispose of it to another government department but without success. Finally it was taken over by Wokingham Without Parish Council. Many of the old huts have been restored and are used by local organisations.

Woolhampton & Midgham

▅▅ When travelling westwards on the A4 (Bath Road) through the village of Woolhampton, you may wonder what the Victorian brick structure is by the turning into Station Road, opposite the Angel Inn. Locally it is known simply as 'The Fountain'.

It was presented to the village by the late Miss Charlotte Blyth who lived at Woolhampton House (now Elstree School). Following an Act of Parliament an artesian well was sunk to provide piped water to the houses in the vicinity of the Bath Road. To commemorate the Diamond Jubilee of Queen Victoria the shelter was erected to house a drinking fountain on the inside wall, and a horse watering trough was provided by the rear outside wall. The inscription over the drinking fountain reads as follows: 'Righteousness Exalteth A Nation – Victoria RI Diamond Jubilee 1897.'

Sadly water no longer flows from the fountain, and the cast-iron animal drinking trough remains empty, but no doubt at the turn of the century this was welcomed by the many horses taken to the once nearby smithy to be shod.

The earliest mill recorded at Woolhampton was in the Domesday Book of 1086. A mill was also mentioned on a document dated 1351, when Philip of Thame, Brother and Prior of the Hospital of St John of Jerusalem, declared John of London free of arrears in rent of a water mill in Woolhampton. (The Knights Hospitallers were the resident lords of the manor from about 1150 until the Dissolution of the Monasteries and the land was bought by William Woolascott in 1544).

The existing mill was built in 1820 with three bays and extended in 1875. It was powered by an undershot water-wheel using the flow of water in the brook run-

148

Victorian drinking fountain at Woolhampton

ning close by into the river Kennet. The Frankum family were the millers for at least over a century; it was last used as a grist mill in 1930.

Now renovated and converted into offices the old mill has taken on a new lease of life, but the once adjacent barns have been demolished.

Brookside House stands on the opposite side of the road to the old mill, known by many locals as 'the Tower House'. It was built by the miller Mr Frankum, it is said as a wedding gift for his son. The tower serves no particular purpose, merely a folly, although rumour suggests that it was built so that the miller could check the sluice gates at the mill from there.

Another idea is that the tower housed a water tank, but this has been discounted by the present owners. The house was the first to have electricity in the village at the turn of the century. The tower is entered from the first floor of the house and contains three small rooms with a narrow staircase winding up between each floor. On the top floor a door opens out on to a flat roof behind, this being surrounded by railings. During Mr George Frankum's occupancy, a flag pole was mounted high on the flat roof, where on all national celebrations or occasions, the appropriate flag would be flown.

Midgham's Victorian letter box was originally located in the front wall of the Coach and Horses public house, but it has now been moved to the side of the lounge bar entrance. The box appears to be the type manufactured by W .T. Allen & Co in the period 1881 – 1904 but the many layers of red paint make it impossible to read the name.

One noticeable difference from more modern boxes is that the posting aperture is slightly smaller. It seems appropriate that this relic of the past remains hidden away here, for at an earlier date the Coach and Horses would most probably have served as the post-house for Midgham and Brimpton.

Lying in the north-east corner of the parish of Midgham is a small tranquil village green. Formerly known as Channel Green, it was the property of the lord of the manor until the final breakup of the Midgham estate, when it was bought by the late Mrs G. J. Brown. She presented it to the village in the care of the Parish Council.

The dip well on the green once supplied the surrounding cottagers with water, the few cottages here dating from the 16th century. The wooden seat was placed on the green to commemorate the Coronation of King George VI, whilst one of the oak trees was planted for the Silver Jubilee of George V. Mrs Brown (the green's benefactress) planted the copper beech tree for the Coronation of Queen Elizabeth II. For the past few years the annual village fete has been held on the green – just one day when it is not so tranquil.

Wraysbury

The village of Wraysbury is in the east of the county on the banks of the Thames, surrounded by green fields and lakes. At Ankerwyke are the remains of a priory, and still to be seen is part of a gatehouse by which the nuns came and went hundreds of years ago.

Magna Carta Island is said to be the place where the charter was signed in 1215. A stone tablet found in the river during the 19th century is kept at Magna Carta House and is reputed to be the table on which King John signed before the Barons.

Perhaps the most interesting building still in use today is the ancient church of St Andrew. There was a

St Andrew's church, Wraysbury

church on the site in Saxon times, though the present
building dates mainly from the 13th century. The font
has been used to baptise the children of the village for
the last 700 years or so, and the carved piscina has served
since the church was new.

In the chancel floor is a stone tablet to Edward Gould,
a servant to Charles II who died 20 years after his
master's long exile had brought him back to the throne.

On the floor of the chancel there are also some interesting brasses. The small one (only nine inches) by the
altar rails is of a youth, John Stonor, the son of a Tudor
squire of Wraysbury. He is portrayed in the habit of an
Eton scholar of the 16th century. History records that he
rose at five in the morning, prayed as he dressed, made
his bed and tidied his room and stood in line to wash. He

began his lessons at six, talked mostly Latin, learned a little Greek, and went to bed at rushlight.

Today there is an ecumenical spirit which unites the parish church and the Baptist chapel, but it was not always so. In 1830 William Thomas Buckland and his wife Mary felt that a decline in moral values and a lack of religious leadership in everyday life called for positive steps. They had started with a Sunday school in 1827, when they purchased two cottages and turned them into one room to house the 25 young scholars – a number that soon increased to 60. The cottage became inadequate and a piece of ground was purchased in 1830 for £45. The first chapel was built and opened on 23rd September of that year. It was called 'Providence Chapel' and the foundation stone, with its inscription, is incorporated in the present building. The total debt of £200 was cleared off in only two years. The chapel was intended from the first to be an alternative for the villagers to the parish church of St Andrew.

The present chapel was opened in 1862. In those days non-conformist chapels were invariably plain and austere, but a pledge of £100 was made on the condition that the new building included some decorative architectural work. The clock tower was added in 1880 and at the same time the building was enlarged. The panel over the door depicts 'The City of Refuge', and Queen Victoria is said to have once stopped her carriage to admire the work.

Index

155